T0361757

Advance Praise for *Scrambled or Sunny-Side Up?*

"At times, we think we need everyone's approval and everyone's praise. But sometimes, just ONE person is all it takes to show you how to believe in YOURSELF! This is one of many powerful gems from the epic love story of Loren and JR told with pure honesty and raw vulnerability through *Scrambled or Sunny-Side Up?*"

~Alicia Keys

"If ride or die were human beings, it would be Loren and JR. I have never seen a more powerful example of how to love someone through thick and thin and to be able to work together while inspiring the whole world. We should all be so lucky to have a relationship like they had.

"Watching them stand back-to-back to protect each other's love and take on the world was amazing to see. This book is so important because it comes from a place of true love, understanding, and survival. Hearing the story behind *Scrambled or Sunny-Side Up?* rained tears in my soul—tears of joy, sadness, and hope."

~Jamie Foxx

"Loren is one of the strongest women I've had the honor to know and love. This heartfelt book explores the intricate tapestry of love, loss, and grief. As you turn each page, you will learn to

honor your emotions, discover hope in even the
most challenging times, and realize that healing
starts with love. Embark on this enlightening
journey and find the strength to turn your pain
into a path toward renewed happiness. This
book is truly a gift to all of us."

~La La Anthony

"I have watched my longtime friends, Loren
and JR, change thousands of people's lives,
including mine. I've learned so much from
them about relationships, business, and even
how to love, which helped me during some of
my darkest times. *Scrambled or Sunny-Side Up?*
is a must-read for anyone who wants to succeed
in all aspects of life."

~Joseph "Fat Joe" Cartagena

"Loren Ridinger's *Scrambled or Sunny-Side
Up?* is a beautiful testament to the strength of
love, even in the face of unimaginable loss. Her
words show us that grief, though deeply painful,
can also be a path to rediscovering ourselves and
becoming our best. It's a powerful and inspiring
journey that resonates with anyone who's loved
and lost."

~Alejandro Sanz

SCRAMBLED or SUNNY-SIDE UP?

SCRAMBLED or SUNNY-SIDE UP?

LIVING YOUR BEST LIFE
AFTER LOSING
YOUR GREATEST LOVE

LOREN RIDINGER

Post Hill PRESS

A POST HILL PRESS BOOK
ISBN: 979-8-88845-808-2
ISBN (eBook): 979-8-88845-809-9

Cover design by TGC Worldwide

This book, as well as any other Post Hill Press publications, may be purchased in bulk quantities at a special discounted rate. Contact orders@posthillpress.com for more information.

This is a work of nonfiction. All people, locations, events, and situations are portrayed to the best of the author's memory. While all of the events described are true, some names and identifying details have been changed to protect the privacy of the people involved.

Post Hill Press
New York • Nashville
posthillpress.com

Published in the United States of America
2 3 4 5 6 7 8 9 10

To those who have lost someone in life who changed their world, who lost themselves as a result but are finding their way back. I'm with you.

To Amber, for showing me how to grant myself grace as I went through it. And for your sacrifice. I saw and felt you put your own life and grief on hold in order to take care of me and others first. You are an amazing mother and incredible daughter. I love you.

And to my grandchildren Ayden, Aydrien, and Ayva—I love you!

TABLE OF CONTENTS

FOREWORD

WHEN I THINK ABOUT JR and Loren Ridinger, I think about two people with an unforgettable love story. They embody love, strength, and resilience. Their bond was unbreakable no matter what test it was put through. It inspired me, and it inspired their friends. It became something we all not only wanted and longed for but were determined to have. I've been privileged to call them friends, share their joys and sorrows, and witness firsthand the incredible partnership they built. JR's sudden passing rocked our worlds in a way that can hardly be described. All of us who knew JR and loved JR watched Loren navigate grief with courage and incomparable grace. This memoir, *Scrambled or Sunny-Side Up?*, is a testament to that journey—a raw, honest, and deeply human story that chronicles their love, loss, and resilience.

Death sucks. But at some point, we will all have to face it. Grief is a part of that process. Grief is a strange and unpredictable beast. You never know how you or someone in your life will react. Nothing truly prepares you for losing someone so vital and integral to your life. It is a wound that takes years to heal and never truly closes. Grief does not follow a timeline; you must let it go on its own time. Some days you scream out in pain; others, you smile in fond memories of the person you knew, loved, and now miss. The truth is that each day is different, and those days can last years, but you learn to deal with them in your own way.

I lost a sister when I was in my early twenties. That was super hard for not only me but my entire family. We were all so vulnerable. One thing I learned is that when you go through challenging experiences that eventually all humankind has to go through, you learn how to comfort others. You know how to be there for them when they inevitably have to go through their grief. You can sympathize much better, have a warmer understanding, and be a shoulder to cry on. One that relates to what they are going through. That relatability is one thing that helps us move on. At some point, we will all experience it; oddly, the fact that others have had to go through these heinous feelings is comforting. When they say misery loves company, maybe this is its meaning. It could have read that misery loves company, but no one wants to be in that company.

These moments of vulnerability have taught me the power of resilience and the strength of community. The love and support of those around me, including Loren, have been a lifeline, helping me rise from the depths of my grief. It's a powerful reminder that we are not alone in our pain, and that the love and support of others can help us navigate even the darkest of times.

Reflecting on this, I often think of my relentless drive to improve. "I'm a perfectionist. I'm pretty much insatiable. I feel there's so many things I can improve on." This mindset of continuous growth has been a cornerstone of my career and life. It's not just about perfection on the tennis court but about striving to improve myself daily. In the context of grief, this drive translates into finding new ways to cope, to grow, and to integrate the memory of my sister into my life in meaningful ways. The loss breaks us down. To piece ourselves back together, we need to actively love ourselves enough to put in the work while understanding that life will never be perfect. It's the everyday trying that counts.

One of the most profound lessons I've learned is the importance of living fully and cherishing our moments with those we love. Life is precious and fragile, and we never know how much time we have. Loren and JR understood this better than most. Their lives, lived to the fullest, serve as a powerful reminder to us all to embrace each moment with gratitude and to live our lives with purpose and passion.

In the early days following JR's passing, I witnessed how Loren drew strength from the community around her. Messages of love and support poured in from all corners, including myself and others who cherished JR and Loren. I remember commenting on Loren's Instagram post, saying, "I am shattered as well for you and with you," fully aware that my words could only provide small comfort in her immense grief. Yet, it was clear that these expressions of solidarity offered her a sense of connection and support during such a difficult period.

Grief has a way of isolating us, of making us feel alone in our pain. But Loren's story shows that we do not grieve alone; we are held up by the love of those who walk beside us. These people hold your hand, listen to your stories, and remind you that you are not alone. As you read *Scrambled or Sunny-Side Up?*, you are not just a passive observer. You are part of this journey, part of this community of love and support.

Loren and I have shared many moments of joy and sorrow. She has been there for me, celebrating my milestones and supporting me through the most challenging times. I met Loren,

JR, and Amber at our friend's house for dinner many years ago. Funny enough, Michael Jackson and his kids were also there. The memories we have shared are incredible. The laughs are even better. Our friendship has always been celebrated amid laughter and love. Loren has often called me her "phenomenal ride or die," a testament to our deep bond. I feel the same.

Her strength in the face of unimaginable loss is a testament to the human spirit's ability to endure and persevere. Loren has courageously confronted her darkest moments, refusing to be defined by them. Instead, she has used her pain as a catalyst for growth and transformation.

In *Scrambled or Sunny-Side Up?*, Loren lays bare the complexities of grief—the anger, the guilt, the relentless search for answers. But she also offers hope, illustrating how love endures beyond the physical world. Her reflections remind us that it's okay to feel lost and to struggle but that healing is possible with time, support, and a willingness to embrace life's imperfections.

Life sometimes throws us what seem to be impossible curve balls, often when we least expect them. We have two choices: we can stay scrambled in the mess of loss, allowing it to consume us, or we can choose to rise, keeping our mind and spirit connected to the bigger purpose in our lives—the sunny-side-up part of living.

In these pages, you will find a story that is both heart-wrenching and inspiring. Loren's words are a gift, a beacon of hope for anyone who has faced loss and wondered how to move forward. She shows us that it's okay not to have all the answers, struggle with the weight of grief, and find our way through the darkness.

Loren's story is not just about losing JR; it's about finding a way to live again, to honor those we have lost while learning to breathe on our own. It's about the power of love to transcend death and continue shaping and guiding us. Loren's story embodies this choice. She chose to find the light amidst the darkness, to honor JR by continuing to live fully and purposefully.

This memoir is not just for those who knew JR; it's for anyone who has ever faced loss and wondered how to move forward. Loren's strength and vulnerability are a gift to us all, providing a roadmap for navigating the labyrinth of grief. I hope her story resonates with you as deeply as it has with me, reminding us that love remains our most significant source of strength even amidst unimaginable pain.

As you read *Scrambled or Sunny-Side Up?*, I encourage you to reflect on your own experiences with loss. Not just loss through death but the lost and found of yourself, which you may be able to identify in many of her lessons. Allow Loren's words to guide you and offer comfort, inspiration, and hope as you navigate your journey. Remember that you are not alone and that a community of love and understanding supports you.

—Serena Williams

CHAPTER ONE

MY LOVE LETTER, HIS LOVE LETTER

My dearest JR,

Like many little girls, I dreamed of falling in love with my Prince Charming. Vivid, almost technicolor dreams washed over me in hues of anticipation and hope. I dreamt over and over again that one day someone would sweep me off my feet just like I'd seen in all those movies like *Pretty Woman*, *The Way We Were*, and *The Notebook*. And in the snap of a finger…just like that…my life would be an endless adventure.

Then, at eighteen, I met you.

The first time I saw you standing across the room, surrounded by a group of people, your laughter ringing out, infectious and bright—I was drawn to you. Your presence was magnetic—an irresistible pull. Your gestures were broad and expressive, your energy boundless. Within five minutes of our first exchange, I threw caution and logic out the window. I wanted to be part of your life and everything you stood for. Even then, when there was nothing to believe in but you, I knew.

There was no money, no company, no home, no car, nothing—not even a plan. Yet my intuition already knew that being with you was a once-in-a-lifetime opportunity to love deeply, work for a creative genius, and be part of a team that could resurrect the great American dream. You stimulated me mentally, always getting me thinking about what was possible. You mesmerized me.

Everything is an incredible and fast ride with you. Remember our first date? You were flying down a road in Greens-boro, going eighty miles an hour. My heart was coming out of my chest, and I grabbed your arm and yelled, "JR, slow down! The speed limit is fifty-five here!"

Your eyes sparkled like a small boy
catching his first tadpole as you said,
"Baby if I had a license, I'd go faster."

Your way of saying "I love you" in those
early days was, "I like you a lot; don't
let it go to your head." I always let
it go to my head!

One of the things I love most about
you is that when I ask you a question
or want a philosophical conversation,
you stop whatever you are doing and
fully engage. Even when I simply need
a definition of a word, you tell me the
definition and then put the word in a
sentence so I can understand it well.
And then, as is your style, you quiz me!
You have been my most excellent teacher,
and that will never change.

You remember that one night, as we sat
under the stars in your beat-up old car,
I asked you, "What's your dream, JR?"

You looked at me with those excited little boy eyes and yelled, "To change the
world, Loren. To help people succeed, to
inspire them to be their best selves."

And I'm so damn proud of you! Watching
you build Market America is incredible.
You're brilliant and resilient, full of
purpose. A billionth of a volt went off
in your mind, and you went nuts with

3

the business. You will make it bigger, but more importantly, you are helping people along the way. You are an architect, engineer, and CEO. You speak all the right languages, bringing thousands and thousands of people in the world together by creating a system that arms people with a weapon to change their lives—a system that allows for time and financial freedom.

You are crazy in the best way and over all these years, you've proven that there is a method to your madness. I've read thousands of letters over the years from employees, entrepreneurs, or even people who never joined the company, and they all detail how you changed their lives, giving them hope and belief. You knew even back then that the only way to change your life is to help others change theirs. This is what visionaries do. You didn't just tell us a new story— you are the living story. What's funny is—I never stopped to think about how much you did the same for me. You gave me confidence and encouraged me when I was unsure or questioned myself—believed in me when I didn't. You made me realize I am enough. Thank you, baby.

We spend every day of our lives together— twenty-four hours a day for thirty-six years, only four days apart when you go skiing. I hate skiing, but you, my dear, are passionate about those black diamond slopes.

What a gift, baby! To know we are meant for each other. To walk through this dream of a life as soulmates.

You once told me, "The only way you can leave me, Loren, is if you stop loving me."

That will never happen.

You always say, "The joy is in the journey." And when it comes to joy, we have Amber. When Amber gave us three beautiful grandchildren, you evolved almost instantly. You reached a new level of being. You always longed to be Pop Pop—you were ready for it. You are a child at heart, and being with Ayden, Ayva, and Aydrien lights you up, and you are their favorite playmate. Your eyes sparkle brighter, and you stop everything when you hear them giggle. If only everyone had a front-row seat to watch you playing shark in the pool, baseball, basketball, having Nerf gun fights, being in the science lab with you, watching you help them build train sets, and catching tadpoles, they would know what it is to feel like you are someone's entire universe.

You and I have fit so many lifetimes into one.

Just two weeks ago, you surprised me again by giving your most extraordinary closing speech at the anniversary of our thirtieth convention. You were transparent and honest, and the crowd loved you for it. Your belief in everyone is incomparable. You're a legend. You left all of you on that stage, giving all of yourself selflessly without expecting to receive. You always, always do the right thing. Your love for people, the business, and your family is a lesson in love.

I didn't only marry you; I married your vision. We all have. You never ask for anything, look for praise, or boast. You just work hard at doing what you love. And most of the time, your worries go unspoken too. I want you to know I see you.

Thank you for being you—for everything you are—your heart, your love, your life—for everything you do, and for showing us what life looks like when you live in the dash.

I was right about you at eighteen—you are my once-in-a-lifetime opportunity. I fell, kept falling, and am still falling madly in love with you more than three decades later. I love you more than life—but what's more important is that you know that.

I know I'm mushy and gushing now, but love is all we truly need—it is all we have ever needed. We are one conscience. Nothing matters without each other.

Every love story is beautiful—but ours is my favorite. I promise you—there will be more magic moments.

I love you—forever.

I believe in you.

Yours always,
Loren

THIS IS THE LETTER I should have left for JR to find one morning as he stepped out of the shower. To read before he shared coffee with me or asked me about his eggs. He wrote me thousands of love letters to discover in various places almost daily. He didn't wait to gush about anything. I saved them all. This is the letter I wish he had read before he so suddenly died.

7

CHAPTER TWO
CROATIA

A Dream Unraveled

"**BABY, DID YOU KNOW CROATIA** boasts over twelve hundred islands, islets, and reefs, but only about forty-eight have people who live there? It's called the Island of Abundance—perfect for us! And did you know it's one of the most diverse archipelagos in the world?"

"What does archipelagos mean again?" I barely looked up from the email I wrote to Marc about everything we needed to handle before leaving on vacation. His enthusiasm pulled me out of my work-focused mindset, but even now, I couldn't fully immerse myself in his joy.

His smile beamed, and his forefinger pointed toward the sky. "Mimi, archipelagos are basically a bunch of islands close together in the ocean. They come from things like volcanic activity." He stood before my laptop, smiling away, intentionally distracting me. I refused to look up and kept tapping the keyboard. "Now use the word in a sentence. Any sentence."

I didn't push back because I'd been right here before. "Croatia is part of a *wild* archipelago where you can sip rum on gorgeous beaches and pretend you don't have a care in the world. Not one. Single thing. To worry about."

He moved away from my laptop and flopped down on the couch, never looking away from me. He was dreaming while awake, as he often did for us. His dreams were a lifeline, pulling us into a world where the stresses of life didn't exist, but I was too buried in my responsibilities to join him fully.

The Island of Abundance

"Ah, c'mon baby. We're going to have a blast. I just read that the cravat was invented there!"

"Cravat?" I slammed down hard on the return key.

"Yes, Croatian mercenaries in the seventeenth century wore a cloth around their necks that caught the attention of the French, who adopted it as 'cravate,' deriving from 'Croat.' They basically invented the necktie!" The twelve-year-old sparkle danced in his eyes.

"And baby, the town of Hum is there. It's in the *Guinness World Records* for being the smallest town in the world with only twenty people. What if we bought island number forty-nine and we moved there with Amber and the kids? Marc, Maria, and Mariah could come too. Maybe Christian, Hunter, and Mekai, and of course Steve and Violet! But that's it! Then we'd be in the *Guinness Book* as living in the smallest town. We could raise a lot of tadpoles there. Wait, let me look up if tadpoles are indigenous to that region." The words fell out of his mouth with an intoxicating rhythm. Normally, I would have drunk in his daydreaming. But Marc and I needed to get on the same page before the trip, so I forced myself to focus on the email, feeling a pang of guilt for not indulging his fantasy.

"Ok, JR. Let me know about the tadpoles 'cuz I think Ayden would love to be a tadpole farmer. Seriously." I hit the backspace button twice. I could sense the tension between JR's carefree planning and my overwhelming responsibilities, and I silently wished I could just let go and join him in his excitement.

Unspoken Fears

My attention was far from Croatia in the weeks leading up to our thirtieth-anniversary conference in August. Marc and I had been meticulously overseeing what would be the biggest, boldest, most important conference of our entire careers. It was August 2022, and COVID was finally waning. People were just starting to tiptoe out of their homes to travel. This was an in-person meeting only, our first in-person event in two years due to COVID. We had to give them a damn good reason—an electric reason—to come to Greensboro. We had to give them every reason to be there. This would be our thirtieth anniversary, and we were introducing the most advanced products and groundbreaking technology yet. Everything was more incredible than ever before, and it was their time—their chance to finally take control of their lives. Being stuck, tired, and frustrated was no longer an option. Now was the time to take action, and we would give them everything they needed to make it happen. Of course, the excitement of Jamie Foxx and Fat Joe performing would make it unforgettable, but beyond the bells and whistles, this was about empowering entrepreneurs to seize the moment.

I almost considered canceling the trip to focus on the conference, but JR's excitement was infectious, and I couldn't bear to disappoint him.

If the hamster wheel, tightrope, and spaceship were JR's biggest stunts before, this thirtieth-anniversary conference would top it all. Everything had to be next level—including the budget. We'd put aside an additional $2.5 million to make this event the biggest ever.

Marc and I spent ten hours a day reviewing every last detail of the conference, down to the color of the tickets. Without a fully staffed events department, the pressure was on us. I was in charge of the music, production, lighting, timing, and order of guest speakers. I arranged seating for our VIPs and family and spent hours shaping and drafting presentations with every single speaker, not to mention my own presentation.

"Are those pyrotechnics going to set the green screen on fire if we have them too close?" I asked one of our producers just as I turned to our caterers. "Make sure we have vegan options for the buffet at lunch," I added, trying to juggle a million details at once.

I tweaked visuals, helped with timing, and sometimes had to tell top-level executives to rip their remarks up and start over. "This is the Super Bowl of Market America conferences," I told one executive. "You need to bring your A+ performance, or you're not getting on stage."

Meanwhile, I was still fully present in my regular role of overseeing all sales and marketing for the company. This included the launch of a dozen new products and helping JR coach and train the entrepreneurs in the field. My phone buzzed nonstop with texts and emails for weeks.

Before leaving for this dream vacation, I had a to-do list a mile long. Oversee the final touches on the new product launch. Haggle with the marketing team about a campaign for a new product. Hire a new social media manager. Confirm logistics for guest speakers. Ensure every last product was in stock for Market America World, our installation next to the main stage. Write my presentation. Review my team's presentations. Help Amber find a contractor for her new house. Review beneficiary documents with JR. Ask Angel to double-check my banking information. Get my clothes together for Jennifer and Ben's wedding and our Croatia trip since we would be leaving right after the conference for both. It felt like I was carrying the weight of the world on my shoulders, and the thought of researching tadpoles native to Central Europe wasn't exactly high on my priority list.

But despite the chaos, there was a part of me that longed for the simplicity of JR's dreams, a part that wished I could escape into his world, even just for a moment.

"Loren! Baby! We're in luck! There are four types of frogs native to Croatia—the common frog, not to be confused with the common tree frog; the agile frog, which is brown, not green like the common frogs—tree or not—and the marsh frog, which can be shades of green and brown but has black spots so we can tell them apart. Hysterically, the common frog is so loud it can be heard from as far away as a kilometer or more! Nothing common about that! Let's build in time off the boat and see if we can find one of each of these little guys! It'll be research for our island breeding habitat…"

"Let's talk about the frogs later. We don't leave for another ten days. I have to wrap things up with Marc and Andrew now, or we're not going to see the damn frogs in peace!" The email had been sent, but I was positive I had forgotten to include a few specific details that would make Marc's life easier while we were on the boat…ten days from now.

A Quiet Foreboding

Croatia had been on JR's bucket list for years. He dreamed of sailing around the Mediterranean on our boat, *Utopia IV*, with Amber and the grandkids. We'd tried to plan this trip several times, but obligations always got in the way. Our boat was now out of commission for months after an oil tanker accident in the Bahamas.

As our twenty-ninth wedding anniversary approached and after hitting our company's thirtieth anniversary, he declared, "We're going!" It was the longest break we'd ever taken to travel around Europe—six weeks—including one week in Croatia. He rented a beautiful yacht for the first part of our trip to sail around Croatia and then we would head to Spain to stay with our very close friend, Grammy Award winner Alejandro Sanz. So that was it. "We're going!"

Unfortunately, Amber and the grandkids couldn't make the first part of the trip but agreed to meet us in Spain. It would be our first major trip without them. Instead, we invited a few friends—my brother Marc, his wife Maria, and our long-time friend Truman. I was actually looking forward to having this time to celebrate us and toast to how far we'd come since those days in our garage building our company from scratch.

In early July, six weeks before leaving for Croatia, JR had his second COVID-19 vaccine booster and a checkup. His blood work was unusual, but he had no symptoms pointing to anything wrong. "It's probably nothing. We can rerun the labs when you return. Go and enjoy!" the doctor said.

"Do you think we should go if there is something up, JR?" I already knew his answer.

"Baby, if I were any healthier, I'd be in the *Guinness Book of Records*! We're going, Loren. It's our time." I couldn't argue with him or the several emails from the doctors encouraging us to go and have a great time.

He had more energy than people half his age and more zest than any human I'd ever met. The only issue was his stiff knee, the result of an old high school football injury, but that was scheduled to be fixed—we were planning to see one of the top sports doctors for the Spanish soccer team Real Madrid while we were traveling through Europe. Alejandro had arranged the appointment for JR after learning about his knee issues. After we got back, he would be in perfect health. His parents lived to 99, and his grandmother was 104 when she died. I was the one who almost died on us in 2015 from a rare brain aneurysm.

"You're right! We're going!" As I agreed, I could feel the sun on our faces already, pushing aside any lingering doubts.

Echoes of Joy

Two weeks before the conference, we got a call from my grandson Ayden. "Pop Pop, I want to go to Disney World for my birthday." Orlando in July was as hot as a furnace, and JR hated extreme heat. Plus, I worried about him navigating the massive theme park on that bad knee. But JR was adamant we go. He wanted to make any wish of his grandchildren come true, and if we had a day to do it, then we would.

Despite the chaos of our schedules, we packed up and flew to Disney World with the kids and a handful of Ayden's friends, determined to make Ayden's birthday unforgettable. We built lightsabers, flew the *Millennium Falcon*, and all the while, JR didn't stop laughing and taking pictures with his grandson. Watching JR's face light up as he shared these moments with Ayden was worth every minute of the scorching heat. Twelve hours later, we got back on the plane and headed home, with a very happy birthday boy and a satisfied Pop Pop, happy to have created another magic moment for the people he loved.

Transitioning back into work mode was a jolt. I hadn't slept more than four hours a night leading up to the conference, but all the hard work, sleepless nights, stress, and logistics paid off at the thirtieth-anniversary conference. The pyrotechnics went off without anything catching fire. The rock-and-roll-themed party we had on Saturday night was amazing. I'll never forget Marc in his leather jacket and eyeliner. Fat Joe and Jamie Foxx performed. Five thousand people came out for that event. I still have the letter JR sent to Marc and me, congratulating us on a job well done.

The Heart of the Storm

But the most special part of the conference was our grandchildren's presence, Ayden, Aydrien, and Ayva. Seeing their wide-eyed wonder at our created spectacle made all the effort worthwhile. They had become our unofficial mascots, charming everyone they met and even getting a shout-out from the stage during one of the keynote speeches. JR's face lit up with pride every time someone mentioned one of their names. As I watched JR from the stage, a deep connection swelled in my chest, and for a moment, everything felt perfect—our family, our work, our life together.

As the conference's final day approached, I felt a mix of exhaustion and exhilaration. We had pulled off the impossible, and the energy in the room was electric. The culmination of months of planning was here, and I could see the impact on everyone's faces—especially JR's. His joy was infectious, and it fueled me to keep pushing through the fatigue.

On the last day, after JR had left the stage and the applause had faded, he took me aside and he was overwhelmed with emotion. He was so grateful and thankful for all that had been done. He could see thirty years being celebrated. He was so thrilled about how all the UnFranchise Owners felt. He saw their faces light up for the three days. It was truly magical! "You did it, baby. You made this conference unforgettable. And look at Ayden, Ayva, and Aydrien—they will remember this for the rest of their lives."

I looked over at our grandkids, who were still buzzing with excitement, and felt a surge of pride and love. All of the kids went crazy. They loved every part of the show, mostly Pop Pop as he would always do crazy stunts and they lived for it. And JR loved that they never left the room when he was on stage, that they loved watching him. This wasn't just about a conference; it was about family and legacy.

As we wrapped up the event, I couldn't help but reflect on the whirlwind of the past few weeks. From the scorching heat of Disney World to the electrifying atmosphere of our thirtieth-anniversary conference, to heading to Savannah to watch Ben and Jennifer become Mr. and Mrs. Affleck—what a rollercoaster just before heading out to Croatia for the long break. But every moment was worth it for the smiles, the laughter, and the unforgettable memories we were creating—especially for JR, our distributors, our family, and the grandkids.

The morning after the grand and romantic affair that reflected Jen and Ben's unique love story, JR and I sat quietly on the deck, sipping coffee and soaking in the calm before our next adventure. "Ready for Croatia?" I asked, glancing at JR, who was gazing out at the horizon with a content smile.

"Absolutely," he replied, his eyes sparkling with anticipation. "But first, let's just enjoy this moment." In that quiet morning light, with the echoes of our achievements still ringing in our ears, I felt a deep sense of gratitude for this life we had built together.

Shattered Reality

And in that quiet morning light, with the echoes of our achievements still ringing in our ears, we did just that.

"Baby, isn't this magical?" JR said to me after we'd finally made it to his personal fantasy island. We arrived in Dubrovnik, one of Croatia's most popular tourist spots, ready to get out and enjoy what was on tap. Stairs weaved around historic buildings, through alleys, and down towards the water, where restaurants and bars lined the waterfront. JR was in a great mood, eager to walk around, pointing out areas he wanted to explore. I couldn't help but feel a twinge of unease as I watched him navigate the uneven terrain, but I quickly brushed it aside, wanting to believe that everything was as perfect as he imagined.

As we strolled around downtown Dubrovnik, scouting the scene, we had to climb up and down several sets of stone stairs with uneven surfaces. I saw JR struggle, as if that knee wouldn't be able to climb. He looked at me, raising an eyebrow in frustration, and paused.

"Baby, are you in pain? Let's go back. We can relax on the boat."

"No, it doesn't hurt, it's just stiff," he said, trying to put on a brave face so we could enjoy our trip. I shook my head as I held his arm. I looked around at the jagged skyline of Dubrovnik, those treacherous stairs and narrow roads leading up and around the town, and wondered if my husband's dream vacation was going to be as wonderful as he envisioned. Despite the growing unease in my chest, I silently vowed to do everything I could to make it so.

The high-wattage sunshine beaming into my room woke me up early the following day. It was warmer than usual that summer in Europe, with nearly every major city reporting record heat. I faintly heard Marc and Truman talking in the kitchen area and the gentle footsteps of the captain and his crew walking around the ship from the top deck. JR and Marc had stayed up until the early morning, shooting the breeze like two young men plotting an epic adventure on a study abroad trip, until Maria and I finally summoned them to bed. But JR was already out of bed, and I assumed he'd be with the rest of the guys. But then the quiet came. I couldn't hear JR's booming voice in the background. It was quiet, and my skin prickled. Pulling on my robe, I went out to the outer deck, which wrapped around the entire lower cabin area. I spotted JR, standing still, staring at the water.

"JR, honey. Good morning. Whatcha doing out here?" I put my hand on the small of his neck. I saw him adjust his knee and wince.

"Good morning, love. I'm just soaking it all in. Isn't this perfect, baby? Just you and me and this sea?"

"Yes. Yes, it is. You feeling okay?" I only asked because I could feel the stiffness in his knee radiating through his body into my fingertips as I gently stroked his hair.

"I'm fine. My knee is acting up a bit. It doesn't hurt, but it's stiff."

I looked out at the open sea. I left him to enjoy the view and the morning air. I went directly to the captain's deck with purpose.

"Good morning, Captain."

"Good morning, Mrs. Ridinger. We'll be docking soon. You and Mr. Ridinger should have a beautiful day exploring the island."

"Captain, I want to get a bike for JR to tour the island. Can you call ahead and arrange it? His knee is acting up, and I think he'll enjoy the sights more if he can bike instead of walk. Can you arrange that?" I looked past the captain to the island, which was becoming more in focus with each moment we spoke.

"Certainly."

Satisfied that I had arranged for JR to explore the waterfalls, I returned to the balcony. JR hadn't moved an inch since I'd left, still staring out at the abyss of the open sea. I stood there momentarily, just watching him, feeling a sense of foreboding that I couldn't shake.

We stopped at Hvar, near Split, and soaked in the scenery and nightlife. Hvar was one of Croatia's many islands, part of an archipelago he so romanticized. Each island seemed to whisper secrets of ancient times and hidden beauty. As we wandered through the cobblestone streets, the warm Mediterranean breeze rustling the olive trees, JR turned to me, his eyes twinkling with joy.

"I'm so happy we're together," he said, his voice soft yet filled with emotion. "I love you. I know how hard it's been to pull off this convention, but right now, we are just going to enjoy our life." His words felt like a promise, but something in his eyes, a vulnerability, made me wonder if he was trying to reassure himself as much as me.

In that moment, surrounded by Hvar's timeless charm, his words felt like a balm to my soul. The stress of the past months melted away, replaced by the simple joy of being together in a place where the past and present intertwined so beautifully.

A Lasting Note

Once on the island, JR and I biked along winding paths flanked by olive trees and vineyards. The salty breeze ruffled our hair. We stopped at a small café for coffee, and he insisted on ordering in Croatian, a language neither of us spoke. The barista smiled, appreciating his effort. We laughed together, sipping our drinks, feeling like young lovers on a spontaneous adventure. In those moments, it was easy to forget the weight of the responsibilities waiting for us back home, to lose ourselves in the simple joy of being together.

That night, I found a note on my bed pillow: Thank you for giving me the bike. It's so amazing. Thanks to you, I was able to see the things I wanted to see. Love you forever, JR.

JR woke up the next morning at 5:30 a.m. "I can't sleep, baby," his voice clear, eyes focused.

I pushed myself up in the bed and turned to him. His hair was all over the place, his T-shirt clinging to one side of his body. The lines on his face detailed every moment we'd ever spent together. Then, as if inside my head, he took the words right out of my mouth. It was as if he could read the fear in my eyes, the worry I tried so hard to hide.

"I love you more than life. You're my best friend."

"You're my best friend too," I replied, feeling a sensation I still struggle to describe even years later, long after the bleeding has stopped. That feeling lingers within me, a mix of curiosity and fear—curiosity to find the perfect word to capture it, and fear of truly understanding its origin. His eyes held mine, and his hands gently moved toward my hips.

"You've made me the happiest person in the world," he said.

I could feel his hands gently tracing the contours of my hips, but his words gripped me by the shoulders, holding me in place, and preventing me from lying back. His touch was tender, but his words were powerful, commanding my entire being. Then, just like that, he laid back down and closed his eyes. I knew he wasn't asleep, just resting. I stayed there, watching him, wanting to memorize every detail, every line on his face, as if I knew, deep down, that this moment was fleeting.

A Strange Request

Stepping out of the shower, I towel-dried my hair and stood at the edge of the bed. "Amber texted. They're scheduled to meet us in Spain tomorrow. I told her that…"

"I don't think she should come," he interrupted. "This is our first trip by ourselves. Let's finish it alone."

I froze, the towel slipping through my fingers. He never wanted to travel without Amber and the kids. Now he was asking me to cancel their visit? It was unlike him. But his knee was acting up, and maybe he didn't want to be less than his best for the grandkids. We only had a few days left; perhaps he was right.

Let's finish it alone. His request was so out of character, it sent a chill down my spine, but I forced myself to nod in agreement, not wanting to upset him.

"I'm going to eat something," he said, a strange weariness in his voice. "I'm not feeling great. Maybe eating will help." I watched him walk out of the bedroom, his familiar stride unchanged, as if he had done it a thousand times. Nothing seemed different, yet everything felt off.

"JR, wait up. I'll come with you, babe. I'm starving." Dropping the towel on the bed, I took long, hurried steps to catch him in the hallway. I felt a growing sense of urgency, like I needed to be close to him, to keep him within my sight.

A Looming Shadow

After breakfast, I got myself ready for the day's excursion. We were in Sibenik to see the famed waterfalls, a highly anticipated stop on JR's itinerary. Even with his stiff knee, he insisted we go. The plan was to take a small charter boat to the island, then get out and walk to the falls for an up-close look. But hiking was out of the question with JR's knee, and we certainly weren't going to leave him behind.

I put on my favorite sneakers for all of the walking we needed to do and grabbed a hat and sunglasses, ready for a day of nature as we prepared to dock in Sibenik. I looked for JR to check on him. Marc and Truman were laughing and talking excitedly, Maria standing next to Marc. I walked past them and looked around for JR. With each step, my heart pounded a little harder, the uneasy feeling from earlier growing stronger.

The morning's heat enveloped me as I walked around the upper deck, finding JR yet again looking out at the water. There was an uneasiness about how quiet he was on this trip. On any other vacation, JR would bounce from room to room, showing off pictures to everyone from his phone that he took at every stop. He would eagerly look up the best places to eat, the most exclusive museums and historical sites, and tell us all where we were going—he usually made maps for people when we were on multi-city vacations, highlighting our designated stops. But now, he was spending a lot of time looking out at the water, pondering life's great questions as if he knew his time was limited. I couldn't shake the feeling that something was very, very wrong.

"Baby?" I said, breaking his concentration. He turned to me with a big smile and walked over, still favoring that knee. "Ready?" he said.

We pulled into the port at Sibenik and gazed at the cascading waterfalls glistening under the sun, the jagged rocks covered in lush, green trees. Long, winding walking paths snaked up the sides of the rocky faces. The view enthralled us.

"I don't think we'll get close enough for a good view," JR said, his face concerned.

"Don't you worry, baby," I said. "Marc and I got it covered." Despite the growing dread in my stomach, I wanted to make this day perfect for him.

When we arrived at the port to board the charter boat, Marc and I quickly approached the charter captain, startling him. "Listen," I said, explaining the situation briefly. "My husband can't walk around too much right now, so you get us as close as possible to those falls so he can practically bathe in the water. Sound good?"

The captain understood the assignment. We boarded the charter and cruised past the other tourist boats, riding right up to the face of the mountain. We never left the boat. The captain had broken all the rules to accommodate my request so that JR and I could see the falls in a way that most people never would. The captain cruised carefully, wiping his brow, looking around for the local coast guard, knowing he could get a ticket driving us this close to the falls. We watched the water rush down, feeling the mist on our faces. JR took my hand and squeezed it gently. They were magnificent—breathtaking. It was his final photo on Facebook. In that moment, surrounded by the beauty of the falls and JR's quiet contentment, I wanted to freeze time, to keep us here, safe, forever.

"I could stay here forever," JR said, his voice soft, almost wistful. His words echoed in my mind long after we left the falls, a haunting suspicion that I tried to ignore.

A Sudden Shift

As we emerged from the falls and reentered the small port, JR was clearly favoring his knee. Without a single complaint, he continued to walk to the boat. But I could see the stiffness had turned into more discomfort. I knew his expressions like the back of my hand.

"I saw a kid walking with a shark tooth on a necklace. I think the kids would love it," he said. "Can you get them? I saw a gift shop off to the right." He pointed to a small shop about five hundred yards away. Nature and animals were important to JR; he loved teaching the kids, so shark tooth necklaces made sense.

"Sure. Meet you back at the boat." I hurried off while he continued to the boat with everyone else.

My phone dinged with a text just as I entered the gift shop. He wrote, "How long will you be?"

"15 min," I replied with a kissy emoji.

"Okay, 1:05 p.m.," the text reply returned almost immediately. He'd never managed my time like that before. I paused for a moment. Why was he concerned about how long I'd be? It was a little thing, but I remember feeling it was odd. I shrugged it off as if he was not feeling well. But that unease, the feeling that something was terribly wrong, wouldn't leave me.

Back on the boat with shark tooth necklaces in tow, we started cruising again, headed towards another stop to dock. JR and I sat in the second-floor lounge area and I took a call with the maintenance team in charge of the repairs on *Utopia IV*. I sat at the dining table near the stairs leading to the lower-level bedrooms. JR sat across from me in a smaller sitting area, listening intently as I led the call with Marc listening in. The maintenance manager from the shipyard was giving me the runaround, talking about delays and additional costs. My frustration grew with each passing minute. JR usually enjoyed listening to me handle these situations, but today he seemed distant and preoccupied. My conversation continued.

Then he got upset, just for a moment, because he saw what I didn't—the guy was bullshitting me. JR was always a man that way, stepping in when he sensed disrespect.

"Don't get upset," I told him. "It's not worth it."

But then, "Why the fuck is it okay for you to get upset, and not me?" he said. He stood up right after that, his breath heavy as he walked past me. I asked him what was going on. He didn't answer.

It was unlike him to leave the room like that. JR never complained, never let on if he wasn't feeling well.

JR briefly touched my shoulder with his hand, a calming gesture. Then I heard him take a deep breath, a raspy inhale as if he were trying to take in as much oxygen as possible and save it up for later. In all the years I've worked beside JR, slept cocooned with him in bed, danced with him, fought with him, or sat beside him while we had our sunny-side-up eggs together, I had never heard that breath come out of him. That sound drew my attention away from the call immediately. My head swiveled toward JR. My heart skipped a beat, a cold dread settling in my chest.

"What's going on with you?" I asked.

"Nothing. Stay here!" he snapped back. He said with a muffled breath as if he were holding his breath and talking simultaneously.

JR loved it when I took charge of things, but sometimes he needed space. His tone made it clear this was one of those times. I stayed put and went back to debating with the boat repairman. But my mind was no longer on the call. It was with JR, wondering if I should have followed him, wondering if I was missing something crucial.

Five minutes later, I was still on the phone with the boat repair guy and Marc. Marc looked at me intensely. He peered around a corner, wondering if JR had gone to the restroom. JR usually loved listening to me work through problems. He would have interjected by now about *Utopia IV*. But he hadn't come back up the stairs. Aware of this, I focused on bringing the call to a close so I could check on him. A growing sense of urgency gnawed at me, the feeling that something was wrong.

* * *

I looked over at the seat JR had been sitting in. We'd hit a steady cruising speed, the boat cutting through the waves of the Adriatic Sea, the wind whooshing around the cabin, producing a tranquil soundtrack. I'd stopped speaking long enough to listen for JR—his footsteps, his voice, anything. The silence was deafening, the absence of his voice like a gaping void

"Marc, stop listening to the call and check on JR," I urged, my voice trembling. Marc went to do so, but then Maria walked in. "JR is on the floor stretching," she said as if it were the most normal thing in the world. I dropped the phone. I screamed.

"JR doesn't stretch on the floor!" Panic gripped me, my mind racing with possibilities, none good.

Marc ran down first. When he came back up, his face was red, panicked.

"He's not breathing," he said.

I ran down after him, but I never made it into the bedroom. Partly because the door was blocked. Inches from him, and I couldn't reach him. And partly because I didn't know if I could face seeing JR in the way I dreaded I would see him.

The world spun out of control. Inside, chaos reigned. Truman and the boat crew were frantically trying to revive JR, performing CPR and using a defibrillator. A doctor, familiar to the crew, was on FaceTime, guiding them through the situation to ensure everything was done correctly since we were out at sea. Intermixed voices and the boat rocking created a perfect storm. My mind was a blur, unable to process what was happening. This couldn't be real. It couldn't be happening.

"Check his breathing! Check his pulse!"

I sat there, curled up like a child, five feet from the door, unable to bring myself to him, listening to their desperate attempts. "We don't have a pulse!" they kept saying. I wanted to run in, push everyone aside, and hold him, but I was paralyzed. I was mumbling, chanting, begging, and praying all in the same breath, "Please, please be okay. It's not time yet. We have so much to do. Please be okay. Please. Please." The words felt hollow, like they were slipping through my fingers, unable to grasp the reality of what was unfolding.

I summoned the courage to get to the bottom of the stairs and be right by his side, but as soon as I inched forward, I heard Truman, forceful and desperate.

"Stay back; he's going to be okay." But I wasn't stupid. Even though I felt like I was underwater with heaviness and fluidity I couldn't control, I could hear everything, and I knew the truth. There was no pulse. JR wasn't breathing. The truth was like a knife to the heart, cutting through the fog of disbelief.

I remember hitting my head against the wall over and over again, "You have to stay with me!" Blood dripped down the side of my face as I continued to hit my head against the wall. The physical pain was a welcome distraction from the unbearable emotional agony.

It didn't matter. None of it worked. Later, the coroner confirmed what I already knew—nothing would have worked.

The Last Goodbye

The paramedics' arms were around me, and I was lifted off the ground and taken upstairs—to the small TV room under the stairs. They sat me in the corner, telling me to stay calm, assuring me that the doctors were still working on him and spoon-feeding me false hope. Their words felt like lies, like they were trying to shield me from a truth I already knew deep down.

Minutes turned into an agonizing eternity. Thirty minutes, maybe forty-five, passed without my awareness. I was at the dock, but I didn't even know it. The weight of my despair was so overwhelming that it drowned out everything else. I sat there, reeling and crying, torturing myself with every possible worst-case scenario, unable to speak, barely able to think. Time had lost all meaning, the world outside that small room ceasing to exist.

I was in such a bad place, lost in my grief and confusion. I didn't realize they had already taken him off the boat. The coroner later told me they had to remove him, but at the time, I thought they were still fighting to save him. The boat crew, Truman, and the others were nowhere to be seen—they were in my room, cleaning up the aftermath so I wouldn't have to face it. I was left in that small room, clinging to false hope, believing they were still trying to bring him back. The reality of his loss didn't hit me until much later, when the shock finally wore off and the full weight of it crashed down on me like a tidal wave.

It was also the first time I heard the coroner say he died from a pulmonary embolism, a blood clot in his knee that likely went to his lungs and killed him. We were days away from getting his knee fixed in Spain. How? The injustice of it all was too much to bear. We were so close to addressing the issue with his knee, and they would have discovered the clot—something we had no idea about. We could have fixed it if only we had known.

And then, the cruelest realization struck me: I wasn't by his side when he left this earth. I didn't get to say goodbye. Or hold his hand. What kind of merciless God would bring soulmates together only to rip them apart in such a brutal way? The pain of not being by his side, of not whispering my love to him in his final moments, was a torment I could barely endure. They were trying to protect me, but all it did was delay the inevitable, devastating truth. JR was gone. I would carry that guilt with me for the rest of my life, a wound that would never fully heal.

Unanchored

On that dock alone, I became truly frozen as everyone ran around me. And then I shattered, collapsing to the floor like glass under a sledgehammer. Pieces of me scattered everywhere, dissolving into the flood melted by my tears. The world around me blurred into a muffled cacophony, like voices underwater. I had become that water, my form disintegrating, bones gone, leaving only a sea of tears. Silent sobs wracked me—perhaps I was gasping, but it all just felt like I was submerged, like a body of water being dragged out to the deep sea. Unanchored. In that moment, I knew I would never be the same again. My world had shattered, and I was drowning in the depths of my grief.

CHAPTER THREE

AFTER THE LIGHT FADES

Held in the Light of Us

THE DAY BEFORE HIS DEATH, I was Loren Ridinger, JR Ridinger's wife. I was also the cofounder of our family businesses, Market America and SHOP.COM, a mother, a grandmother, a sister, and a friend. Three months after his death, I was hopelessly confused about my eggs.

After sludging through another night where I could only sleep in forty-five-minute increments, I dragged myself through the morning. Making sure my hair and makeup looked good even though I felt terrible, I tried to mentally prepare for a long string of Zoom calls with my senior leadership teams. Entering the kitchen, I poured a cup of coffee, taking a swig without caring if my lipstick smudged. Standing in the kitchen, staring at the stove, I heard his voice:

"Mimi, scrambled or sunny-side up?"

It was such an absurdly simple question. The memory seemed to float through the sunlight, hanging in the air like the steam rising from my coffee. His voice came to me daily, so I wasn't startled. In some ways, I was more resigned. I could hear his voice but couldn't have him with me. I chalked it up to his way of staying connected, even when he was gone.

For as long as I can remember, JR would wake up every morning and insist we do two things together: stay in bed a little longer and have breakfast. Given our three decades together, it may seem unbelievable, but hands to sky, it is the truth.

JR always teased me about how I'd leap out of bed, ready to dive into the day without a second thought.

"Good morning, Mimi," he'd say with that infuriatingly casual smile. I would kiss him, smile, stretch, and climb out of bed.

"Don't rush," he'd say. "Let me have you for just a few more moments." The way he'd say it, his voice low and gentle, it always felt like he was trying to hold on to time itself—like those moments were our little pockets of eternity. He wanted a few more shared moments of our pillow talk. More often than not, I'd brush it off, always in a hurry, continually moving.

Then, again, he would find me every morning to have breakfast before the day took us along for a ride. He'd sit at the table, stretch his legs, and let the sunlight pour over his face like he was soaking in some quiet, unspoken truth. I'd look over sometimes and see the sun casting a halo around his head. Some days, it made me laugh; others just fueled my annoyance over our egg conversation.

Without fail, he'd ask, "How should I have my eggs today? Scrambled or sunny-side up?" It was one of his many love rituals, curated over decades together. Some days, it drove me up the wall. It was just eggs. But the man had a way of turning the mundane into a kind of daily ceremony as if the ritual held the threads of our life together.

"JR, why do you always ask me that? I'm busy. Have them the way you want them!" I'd shrug off, half-dressed, eyes glued to my phone, scrolling through emails and messages.

He'd just chuckle, unfazed. "C'mon, Mimi, scrambled or up?"

"Scrambled," I'd giggle, barely looking at him.

"Great. But I'll wait until you're ready to have breakfast with me." Looking up from what I was doing, I never knew if I should be overcome by his romantic antics or annoyed by his cavalier attitude towards my own morning routine.

"Okay, JR, baby. Coming. Let's have some eggs." It didn't always play out like that, but I often gave in to his infectious nature, mainly because it included his desire to have me near him.

He'd nod, content, and go about getting breakfast ready, the smell of sizzling butter and eggs filling the kitchen. In these small, seemingly inconsequential moments, the enormity of what we built—the business and our lives—became the most apparent. The light from those mornings now feels distant, like it faded with him, taking some part of me with it. It all seemed so solid, so permanent.

But that was before.

Lost in the Everyday

Months after what should have been our first vacation without the kids—months after finding him lifeless, face up, just passed the stairs, in the bedroom on the yacht we had chartered in

Croatia—I finally began to understand why those eggs gnawed at me. It hit me like a punch, the memory of his body—so still, so heavy, in a place where life should be bright and boundless. On this particular morning, staring at the stove, grief hit me like a wave, suddenly and all at once, the way grief does when it catches you off guard. I realized that amid the banter about scrambled or sunny-side up, those quiet moments had become the heartbeat of my mornings. Without him, the silence was deafening. His absence unbearable. Every morning now begins with that same silence, the kind that stretches into everything—like the world is hollow. The egg carton sat unopened on the counter, a mundane object that now felt like a weight pressing down my chest. Why didn't I see it when he was still here? The eggs weren't about breakfast. They were about us. They were about a life where something as small as choosing how your partner likes their eggs created an unbreakable bond.

When we first got together, I loved how JR asked my opinion about what seemed like every little thing. Every single little thing! He went out of his way to ensure I knew he valued my opinion, even in trivial things. But as the years passed, the sweetness of the ritual wore thin. Running a business, raising a family, managing everything—it left me with no room for small decisions. Now, I can see that those "small" decisions were anchors, grounding us in a world of chaos. But grief can make even the smallest choices feel monumental—because without him, nothing felt stable. It's strange how the pressures of life can crush the things that used to feel light, like choosing eggs or laughing about something silly. Those small decisions—decisions I wish I could be annoyed by just one more time—make all the difference. But things that once made me smile became things that grated on me, not because of the acts themselves, but because life was pressing in from every side. With the last swallow of my coffee, I acknowledged a hard truth: the things you fall in love with—the quirks, the rituals—are the same things that splinter you when they're gone.

No one warns you about losing the little things. Grief is in the details. In ordinary events, the aftermath of loss feels insurmountable because the person who made them meaningful is no longer there. Now, those quiet moments of conversation over breakfast, the shared silence broken only by the clinking of cutlery, are gone. The silence is so thick some days, it feels like I'm wading through it, grasping for anything that will break it—anything to fill the void. There's nobody to collect my opinions like precious stones.

The mornings were sacred—our time. Before the chaos of running a multimillion-dollar empire, there was breakfast: simple, predictable, grounding. It was a ritual that, in its steadiness, seemed to hold our world in place. But after losing my greatest love on that open ocean in Croatia, that same predictability felt suffocating. The kitchen that once felt alive with morning light and movement now felt too still, like time had stalled. The routine that once brought us together now created an undefinable space between us.

That conversation about how he wanted his eggs—dear God, it used to get under my skin. But if I'm honest, the man sitting across from me, sipping his coffee and smiling at whatever was on his plate, defined me more than I realized. There was something about his presence that made the world make sense, something that made even the smallest rituals feel like they had weight—like they held everything in place. He pulled something out of me—a depth of integrity, a heart I didn't know I had. He turned me into a leader, a partner who could build an empire alongside him. I was *his*—part of every title he held: his wife, partner, Amber's mother. And "Mimi"—the name he gave me after the grandchildren were born—became more than a nickname. I was Mimi to Ayden, Aydrien, and Ayva—their grandmother. But he began calling me Mimi more and more until it just became second nature. I can still hear him saying it, like a whisper that lingers in the spaces he used to fill. It marked a shift in our lives, a new chapter where I evolved in his eyes. It was our evolution. Without JR, I felt like I was drifting, unanchored, staring at the stove, wondering what the hell I was going to do next.

Clinging to the Familiar

Three months after losing him without any warning in Croatia in August 2022, I was still wrestling with the simplest of decisions. I was still stumbling through each day, trying to make sense of a life that now felt unrecognizable. What should I eat for breakfast? The most minor things hold the world's weight when you're barely holding on to yourself. Deciding between scrambled eggs and an omelet became a mental battle I could not fight. The effort it took to decide what to have for breakfast outweighed any other responsibility I had. I couldn't focus on running a business, playing with my grandchildren, or planning my day until I'd made peace with what would be on my plate. The things that used to be routine now feel like mountains, impossible to climb without him there to help me navigate.

Why didn't I understand about the damn eggs sooner?

In the early days of Market America, it was just the two of us—dreaming, building, surviving. Back when our lives were chaotic and cluttered with papers, coffee cups, and dreams, we scribbled down ideas that only made sense to us in the middle of the night. We didn't have money, resources, or connections; it was just JR's unshakable strength and faith that we could transform an idea into something that could change lives. He was eighteen years older than me, but we were equals when it came to our determination. While I worried about what people would think about our age difference, JR was never concerned.

"It doesn't matter what they think, Loren; it only matters what you and I think."

He was the dreamer and the visionary, and I was the one who made sure those dreams had unlimited support and enthusiasm to come true. I cared for JR in many ways and loved being "his girl." We worked side by side, inseparable—boyfriend and girlfriend, lovers, business partners, and eventually husband and wife, chasing a vision that felt impossible until it wasn't. He was and forever will be the love of my life, my soulmate, the one who could see the world not as it was but as it could be.

Over time, that dream became real—it became a billion-dollar empire spanning nine countries, creating opportunities for people who, like us, just needed someone to believe in them. But it wasn't the success that bound us. It was the love that deepened when we built something together from nothing, when we weathered storms, and when we celebrated victories side by side. It's that love that I still feel, even in the moments when the pain threatens to drown me. That love is like a tether, holding me even when I feel like I'm floating away—lost in the waves of grief. That love made the most minor rituals carry the weight of something sacred.

Without JR at the helm of Market America, everything felt unsteady—both in my mind and at corporate headquarters. The revenue began slipping, millions disappearing as if the foundation we'd built was crumbling under the weight of his absence, coupled with the world recovering from COVID-19 and technology changes. It was on me to stop the bleeding, to step in, plug the holes, and steer everyone in a new direction. But how do you steer a ship when you've lost the compass? When the one who always knew the direction isn't there to point the way? The days blurred together, a thick fog clouding my vision. I moved forward, but I felt directionless, untethered, without the man who was our North Star for so, so long.

At work, the team walked on eggshells, offering love and support that only served to remind me how fragile everything felt. I saw the worry etched across their faces—the way their eyes flickered with concern during every Zoom call, the way they exchanged glances in the hallways when they thought I wasn't looking:

"Is she okay?"

"Will she be okay?"

"Can she really pick up where JR left off?"

"Does she even want to?"

"Will she snap out of it?"

"She doesn't need to do this. She could walk away and live comfortably for the rest of her life. Why would she put herself through this?"

"Some people just don't recover."

"We love her, but…"

I couldn't tell if these were their thoughts or the shadows of my doubts echoing back at me. But it didn't matter. I stared at the computer screen, the cursor blinking, frozen mentally in the same place I was when I walked into the kitchen. The Zoom calls had started. My thoughts lingered in the spaces between tasks. In these moments, I should have focused on running the company, but I found myself stuck in making the most trivial decisions, like making a dentist appointment this week or waiting until next week.

I knew I couldn't keep turning away from the business, no matter how much grief tried to drown me, to pull me under. This wasn't just about me—it was about us, the legacy we built together, JR's vision, and the livelihoods of thousands of people worldwide. But grief is a thief, robbing me of the clarity and drive I once took for granted. Even as I stood at the edge, knowing that the leadership of Market America was mine to take, I was paralyzed by the weight of it all, the loss pressing in from every side. How do you carry on a mission when the one who made you believe in it is gone? The world expected me to step up and continue our mission together. But in those darkest moments, I couldn't see beyond the void his absence.

I was conscious of the fact that three months after his death, I was still unable to face mornings alone. The world was moving on, and I was expected to move with it, but the truth was, I was still struggling to move past the stove each morning.

"Good morning, team. Let's get started." I began my first meeting of the day with sheer will and a strange accountability to JR that I still didn't understand.

What Remains after Goodbye

My Zoom calls unfolded into frustrating, angry discussions that put everyone on edge. I lost it. I fought with everyone—Marc, my brother and president of Market America; Steve, my other brother and president of SHOP.COM; Christian, a vice president; and even my sweet daughter Amber who also worked for the company. I fought over things that didn't matter—timelines, details, decisions that would usually be routine. I was lashing out because it was easier than facing the truth—I didn't know how to be the leader everyone needed me to be without JR by my side. The pressure to be everything at once—to be the one everyone looks to for answers—became unbearable when the one person I always looked to was gone. By 3 p.m., I had all I could stand and decided to retreat to my home in Connecticut just to be alone.

After the blow-ups, Amber texted, asking if she should come over. I told her no. I just wanted to curl up in my green sweatpants—the ones no one ever sees me in—and shut out the world. I wanted to sink into the loneliness that felt like drowning.

The drive home was long and silent, each passing mile a reminder that JR wasn't waiting for me at the end of it. We bought this house in 2018—our sanctuary, our escape from the world we built. It was a place where we could just be Loren and JR, not the cofounders of Market America or the business power couple that people saw us as. But now, the house felt like a museum, where everything was preserved, frozen in time, but empty of life. The rooms that once echoed with laughter now only carried the echoes of what used to be—ghosts of moments that no longer had anyone to inhabit them. I stepped inside, and it was like walking into a past life—one that was haunting me with every memory etched into these walls.

Now, it was just me, trying to figure out what to do next. I dropped my purse by the entryway, the sound echoing. I headed straight to my closet and changed into those green sweatpants. It was impossible to walk into that closet without seeing JR's things still hanging there, perfectly arranged just as he liked. I still can't bring myself to move anything. Every shirt and pair of shoes is a reminder that he was here, that we shared a life.

I left the bedroom and dragged myself into the living room; the sun setting, casting long shadows across the room, making everything feel emptier and more distant. It was like the light in the house was different—duller, like it was just going through the motions, just like I was. I flipped through the channels, not seeing what was on the screen, just looking for something to fill the silence. I landed on *Friends*. JR would laugh at me for watching reruns of a show I've seen a hundred times, but something was comforting in the familiarity of it. I settled in, hoping it would distract me from the ache gnawing at me all day. Ross and Rachel laughed and bantered while I sat numb, hoping their joy could replace my ache.

But the mail caught my eye—a pile I'd been avoiding. I told myself I'd get to it later but knew that was a lie. I just didn't want to face what was in there, especially not the envelope addressed to "Mr. & Mrs. Ridinger." The name stung—both a reminder of what was and what was lost. It was a wedding invitation, and seeing those words hit me like a punch to the gut. The words blurred as tears rose, and the "Mr." stared back at me coldly. How would I respond to something like this? How do I RSVP when half of that "we" is gone? I couldn't cross out his name. I couldn't bring myself to pretend like I was just "Loren Ridinger," as if being JR's wife was just a role I played that I could step out of now that he was gone. It feels like being "Mrs. Ridinger" is all I have left of him, all that keeps the connection alive. I realized that while I still had his name, all those other little things connecting us had disappeared like the foam on a wave.

I dropped the envelope and let myself sink deeper into the couch. Ross and Rachel on the TV were oblivious to my pain—Ross was whining about something, Chandler was cracking jokes, and the theme song blared in the background, mocking me with its upbeat cheerfulness:

"I'll be there for you…"

But he's not. He's not there for me. And no matter how many times I heard that stupid song, it only reminded me how much I hated the world for moving on without him.

The tears came, uninvited, spilling over as I screamed at the TV, the empty room, and the universe. "Where the fuck are you, JR? Where are you?"

The anger welled up, turning into this searing, raw ache in my chest that I couldn't soothe no matter how hard I tried. The anger turned to panic. Panic into isolation. It was like I was trapped inside myself, screaming for someone who wasn't there to hear it anymore. I wanted to throw something, break something, anything to match the brokenness inside me. But instead, I just sat there, sobbing.

I was crying so hard I couldn't breathe, my throat raw from shouting, my heart shattered all over again. I finally fished the remote from under the couch and turned off the TV. The silence was my constant companion. I stood there, clutching that stupid wedding invitation, wondering again how to move forward.

And then it happened. The pain in my back molar exploded in my head. It had been throbbing for a week, a dull, nagging pain—just another reminder of all the varieties of hurt that had settled in since JR died. But in an instant, I was ripped from my grief and thrown into a battle with nerve-drilling pain that made my jaw and my head vibrate with excruciating force.

The Weight of Labels

I pressed my hand against my cheek, trying to soothe the relentless ache radiating from my back molar. The dentist's office greeted me with a blast of cold air, sending goosebumps racing down my arms. The antiseptic smell curled into my nostrils, mixing with the distant hum of a drill—a sound that felt like the prelude to something far more final than a filling.

The receptionist, a kind woman with brown hair who'd known me for years, handed me the clipboard with a polite smile. I caught a flicker of something in her eyes—a glance that felt too familiar, that same look I'd seen on strangers, one that seemed to say I was missing something vital. Like I'd run out of the house half-dressed. Maybe that's how they saw me—a woman stripped bare by loss.

I took the clipboard in one hand while my other hand absentmindedly rubbed my aching cheek. It was another lovely day in the "Let's Pretend Loren is Fine" club. The world keeps spinning, and I'm supposed to pretend I'm okay while I'm barely holding myself together. I sank into one of the stiff chairs in the waiting room, my body heavy with the kind of exhaustion that sleep doesn't fix. On the wall, the TV blared an episode of *Hoda and Jenna*. Their bright outfits and cheerful banter felt like a cruel mockery of the world I was living in. I glanced down at the clipboard, at the irritating forms that had become another relentless chore in the aftermath of JR's death.

Death certificate. Notify Social Security. Insurance claims. Banks. Credit bureaus. Government agencies. Estate and probate. A mountain of documents, signatures, phone calls, and meetings. In triplicate. It was like my life had become a checklist—one where I kept crossing off the pieces of everything we

43

built together. The list of tasks felt endless, each a fresh reminder that he was gone, that everything we'd built together was now a pile of paperwork to be sorted and filed away. And that was just for our personal life. The business—Market America and SHOP.COM—came with towering responsibilities that felt even heavier without him.

I stared at the clipboard, scanning the repetitive questions. I'd been coming to this dentist for years—didn't they already know these details by heart? My birth date, my address, and the date of my last cleaning. A few months ago, I couldn't even remember basic information like that—my mind was stuck in the haze of grief, unable to recall anything beyond Croatia. Today, I could finally remember the details; maybe that was progress—small victories in a battle I never signed up for.

I clicked the pen and started at the top.

Name: Loren Ridinger. I've been Loren Ridinger for thirty-six years. I was, and always will be, Loren Ridinger. I felt tight in my chest as I wrote my last name, a flicker of JR's face flashing as I spelled out "—inger." My hand stiffened, but I pushed through, forcing the letters onto the page.

Phone number: area code, seven digits. I scribbled them down quickly before they slipped away. It's not like I ever answered the phone these days, anyway.

Then I reached the part that made everything inside me freeze: three little boxes demanding I define myself.

Married. Single. Widow.

Those words felt like they were mocking me, like they could somehow contain the complexity of everything I've lost. The throbbing in my tooth surged like a spike driven straight into my jaw. I dropped the pen onto the clipboard, staring at those words as if they could somehow alter the reality of my situation.

Box 1: Married.

I was married the last time I came here. I am still married. I didn't get a divorce. I didn't leave him. I'm still devoted to my husband.

Box 2: Single?

Single, like never married? Single, as in currently not married? I don't feel single. I felt…untethered.

Box 3: Widow.

The word curled my lips in disgust. It sounded like wilted flowers left to rot on a forgotten grave, like something weak and lifeless. Widow. That label felt so wrong, so small, compared to the enormity of what I'd lost. How can a single word define a relationship that spanned decades, built empires, and was filled with love that still echoed in every corner of my life? My marriage was more than a checkbox. It was a life, a partnership, an endless love story. How do you reduce that to a single tick in a box?

What about adding boxes for heartbroken? Devastated? Alone? Or even undecided? Maybe they should add "Emotionally Wrecked" as an option.

I hovered my hand over the page, but I couldn't make contact with the paper. I couldn't choose any of these labels. They didn't fit. Losing JR isn't a box you can tick. And since when does my dentist need to know my fucking relationship status?

I set the clipboard down and left the form unfinished.

"Mrs. Ridinger?" A voice called from the examination room. I stood up, purposely leaving the clipboard behind in the chair. Let them figure out my marital status from the X-rays. Maybe they'll get a clue from how I've been grinding my teeth at night. I walked into the exam room; my jaw clenched, both from the throbbing pain and the stubborn refusal to fit into the boxes someone else decided for me.

The dentist confirmed what I already knew—I had a cavity. "We can schedule you next week if you like," the receptionist said. The clipboard was back beside her, my half-completed form glaring at me from the counter. I swallowed down the tear threatening to escape and simply shook my head. "No. I'll call you when I'm available." I could live with the pain—after all, it was just one more on a growing list. But I couldn't face those damn checkboxes again. It wasn't lost on me that I was being irrational. But I didn't care.

Back in Greenwich, I walked into the living room, dizzy and disoriented. The painkillers had kicked in. Then, through the fog, my eyes locked onto the coffee table, zeroing in on the wedding invitation that had been sitting there, ignored for days. I picked it up, still holding my aching cheek, and felt a new wave of confusion.

Am I still Mrs. JR Ridinger if JR isn't here?

I bit my lip, my mind juggling questions I didn't know how to answer. Am I still a Mrs.? Or am I now Ms. Ridinger? The woman formerly known as Mrs. Ridinger? What's the correct protocol for this? Of course, I'm still fucking married! I'm always going to be JR's wife. I threw the invitation back down, a mix of frustration and defiance bubbling up inside me. How can a piece of paper tell me who I am? I'm still who I was—we're still who we were. He didn't leave me; he passed away. But then I saw another envelope I'd ignored. I tore it open and felt my heart drop.

A few hours later my lawyer called—the nail in my day's coffin.

He informed me that my marriage had been terminated. Under Florida law, death automatically ends the marriage—no more obligations, no more benefits. Just like that. Florida decided my marriage was over without even asking me.

But he's always going to be with me. Right. Right?

I let the envelope fall from my hand. There would be no resolution today. These are questions with challenging answers. And maybe they're not questions that need answers at all.

Love's Lingering Echo

Later that night, back at home, I sat at the kitchen table, staring at a blank piece of paper. I started writing, almost without thinking:

```
Dear JR,

The answer is sunny-side up. I'm sorry
for every time I got frustrated when
you asked me how you should have your
eggs. I know now that it wasn't about
the eggs—it was about us. If you could
ask me again tomorrow, I'd tell you
sunny-side up. Every time.

                    I love you forever,
                         Loren.
```

The tears that came this time were softer, like the grief had been consoled, even if just for a moment. The tears came again, but they were softer and less angry this time. Grief is strange like that. It's not always the sharp edges and gut-wrenching sobs. Sometimes it's quiet—a soft embrace covering every inch of your body, reminding you that you've lost something irreplaceable. I folded the letter and left it on the table as if maybe he'd find it in the morning like he always did.

But he wouldn't.

The Lesson: When Love Outlasts Loss

As I climbed into my side of the bed with heavy eyelids, it occurred to me that it was impossible to grieve this hard without having first loved JR even harder. The weight of the grief, the way it feels like drowning in a relentless tide, is only this unbearable because the love we shared was just that immense. It's like the grief is a shadow—looming large because the love that cast it was so bright. And while I didn't know how to climb out of this grief, while every day felt like I was treading water with no shore in sight, I realized that I was only slowly drowning in it because the love we had before he died was stronger, more significant, more alive than anything grief could ever take away from me now.

Grief is an extension of love. The deeper you love, the deeper you grieve. It's the shadow side of what was once light. And even though it's suffocating and feels like it's pulling you under, there's a strange comfort in knowing that this pain is the flip side of a boundless love that shaped who I am. Grief, as unbearable as it is, doesn't diminish that love. It proves how fully and fiercely we loved while we had the chance. Now, life was about living in the after.

I might not know how to control grief, but I do know this: the love we had, the life we built, is bigger than the pain of losing it. Realizing this kept me afloat, even when I couldn't conceive of going on.

And that's the lesson—grief only exists because love was there first. And that love, even in its absence, is still a light to hold on to, still guiding me through the darkness   even when I can't feel it. And that love, even in its absence, still has the power to support us, keep us fighting against the tide, and remind us that the love we share is stronger than anything death can ever take away.

CHAPTER FOUR

CRACKING
UNDER PRESSURE

The Weight of Loss

I LAY CRUMPLED AT THE foot of the bed, clinging to the sheet they had forgotten. JR's sheet—the one they laid him on while they tried everything to bring him back. The soft, cream-colored sheet now bore the weight of my despair. My cheek pressed against it, my hand clenching its corner, and I noticed tiny drops of dried blood tangled in my hair, but I didn't move. I just lay there, holding on to the last tangible piece of him.

Then I heard Truman's voice from upstairs.

"Loren, Loren, get up here." His voice cut through the haze, but I barely lifted my head, straining to see up the stairs without moving the rest of my body. "Loren, you'll never believe it. After they took him off the boat, they tried one last thing and—oh my God, Loren. He's back. He's alive. Get up. He's asking for you."

JR was alive?

The hope was a cruel slap that jolted me awake, only to be yanked back into the relentless reality that he was gone. Those days after getting off the boat in Croatia, I was caught in a cycle of false hope and brutal truth. Being awake meant I wasn't torturing myself with impossible dreams, but it also meant replaying every moment, every detail, like a detective obsessed with solving a crime.

"Your husband passed away peacefully...he didn't even know it was his last breath," the coroner assured me.

"Prove it. How do you know it was peaceful?" I demanded, desperate for any piece of information that could make sense of this nightmare.

I interrogated everyone—from the captain to Truman, Marc, Maria, and even the chef. Over and over, I asked the same questions, searching for something, anything, to make sense of it. I even wrote to the Croatian ambassador. No one was safe from my inquisition.

In those hellish days, I moved through the motions, not by choice, but by some force beyond myself. Minutes after we docked, the reality of JR's absence set in, as if invisible strings took over, guiding me through the "had-to-be-dones."

One Day AJRD (After JR's Death):

We had to address the world. JR was a leader to thousands, and rumors were already swirling. The board for Market America and SHOP.COM needed explanations. Some said JR had fallen off the boat, which was a wild fabrication we needed to correct immediately. But the most challenging part was Amber. She was in the Hamptons with the kids, and I couldn't let her hear it from the gossip columns or strangers. We didn't want her to find out like that. Someone she trusted had to be there to tell her the crippling news and hold her up when she most certainly would crumble. I couldn't be there, but I could send one of our own to the Hamptons.

I coordinated with our estate manager Angel to be there when the call came in. We needed him to reach her first. The kids were in the Hamptons Classic, still competing. She was in the crowd, the kids still on their horses. We waited for them to finish, for her to be somewhere private. But there wasn't time. Angel flew from the city in a helicopter, but by the time he landed and the kids were in the car, the news was already slipping out.

Marc had to make the call. He used my phone. When she answered, she thought it was me, that something had happened to me. But it wasn't me. "It's your dad," he said, and I heard her and the kids fall apart. I was in the corner of the room, on the floor, and when he told her, I screamed. I wanted him to stop talking, to not say the words that couldn't be unsaid. I could hear their screams through the phone.

All the while, I was on the boat, guiding the board of directors as we crafted the statement to the world. My brother Steve ultimately wrote it with my input, but every word had to carry the weight of truth. We timed the release ideally—Amber needed to know first to prevent the rumors from spiraling further. When Amber knew the truth, I collapsed back into Loren, who had all her strings cut.

The next morning, I started visiting JR at the funeral home and stayed with him every day. I would bring a change of clothes for him, brushed his hair, and sat with him. I wasn't going to let him out of my sight. I know people were worried about me, but I knew that I was better there being with him. I was just waiting for the ambassador to call and tell me when we could go home. She was incredible, working behind the scenes, but no one knew how long it would take. Everyone was calling—David Beckham, Victoria Beckham, Alejandro Sanz, city councilmen, governors, senators—trying to get me out of there. At Amber's request, Alejandro flew to Croatia to be with me and Marc to help in any way he could.

On the third day, as I went to be with JR at the funeral home, I encountered an elderly woman, equally consumed by grief but visibly angry. She was there to sign the burial papers for her husband. Her sobs reverberated through the stillness, and in that moment, the rawness of her sorrow reflected the ache in my own heart, as if we were both drowning in different shades of the same pain.

She cried in a way that was different from anything I had heard—a guttural, broken sound that was hard to listen to but impossible to ignore. When I gently asked her how her husband had died, she told me it was from a heart attack. Her voice trembled as she explained that her tears weren't just for his death but for the years they had spent apart while he worked and for the moments they could never reclaim. They had been married for over forty years. She was aching. It was their first trip away, a wedding, and she was older than me—angry too. Angry that they'd never taken the vacations they planned, never did the things they said they would. For a brief moment, I felt thankful. JR and I had done everything together. We didn't have those stretches of time apart. That's why her cry sounded different—like regret, something I would never know. Guilt, maybe, but not regret. It was the sound of a life half-lived, and it hurt to hear. But I also felt relieved, grateful even, because we didn't have that.

But as the sense of gratitude settled and I sat with that realization, the weight of the present began to creep back in.

The woman's sorrow lingered in my thoughts as I faced the harsh reality of our situation. The practicalities of death loomed large.

By day five, they called to tell me I could take him home. It was unheard of to leave by day five, but that's what happened. They would meet me with him at the private airport.

When we got to the plane, it hit me. I sat there, waiting to take off, holding a folder they'd given me—inside were JR's death certificates. Fifteen copies, they told me. "You'll need them when you get home." There was also a letter for the secretary of state, paperwork I had to sign upon landing. I sat in that corner of the airport, alone, in disbelief. I couldn't wrap my head around it. JR had wanted to come here so badly, and now I was leaving with him in a body bag. A fucking body bag.

Then came the worst part—they told me he wouldn't fit on the plane in the hard case. I don't know what it was, some kind of coffin, I guess, and they couldn't fit it. They suggested putting him in cargo. I refused. I told them to take him out of that box and put him right on the couch. I didn't care how crazy I sounded. I said I'd do it myself if I had to. The pilot, bless him, said, "Let me do this for you." He promised to get us both home.

He placed JR on the front couch and told me to take the back one. Every time Marc and Maria fell asleep, I'd sneak up to the front. I just couldn't leave him alone.

On the plane ride back, I whispered to JR in those quiet hours, finding a tiny droplet of peace in knowing we were making the final journey side by side.

When I landed, it was the middle of the night, around 4 a.m. I remember we had to change airports because there was press waiting at the first one, so we diverted to JFK. When we touched down, Amber was there but not the babies—along with Duane, and some state officials waiting to handle the paperwork. They took JR off the plane first. I stood there, watching as they took him away for the first time. They placed him in the hearse, and I'll never forget how Amber walked over, touched him through the plastic for a brief moment—just a touch—then got into the car with me.

It was early the next morning, maybe two hours later. By the time I got home, I had barely slept. I went downstairs and found Angel and Marc on the phone. There was a problem with JR's body. They handed the phone to me, and that's when I was told—he didn't look like he'd been embalmed.

He said JR didn't look like he had been embalmed because he was already deteriorating. There were entry points where they had tried to perform the procedure. At that moment, I knew there was a severe problem. An investigation revealed that the clot preventing the embalming fluid from flowing through JR's body was much bigger than anyone had realized.

I called the funeral director in Croatia, who explained that he had only seen such a complication in people who had received a vaccine booster from America and a few other places. The clot was so big, long, and stringy that the fluid couldn't properly flow through JR's body. They had done their best to embalm him, but it wasn't enough. Despite their efforts, JR was already starting to deteriorate by the time we landed.

They signed off, knowing. They had to—otherwise, I couldn't bring him home. It's the law. The body has to be embalmed to fly. So, they did it. Signed the papers, even though the embalming hadn't been done properly. In the end, they did me a favor.

At least we were finally home together.

Two Months AJRD: Unraveling the Threads

Days turned into weeks, each blending into the next, a blur of grief and the numbing monotony of routine. I floated through it all, disconnected as if watching my life from afar. But then came a moment that pierced through the fog, demanding my attention.

I found myself standing in the middle of our bedroom, JR's cell phone in one hand, mine in the other. Their weight was astonishing, as if these small devices carried the full burden of our shared life—our love, laughter, arguments, and history. A wave of panic crashed over me, a sudden realization that I was holding evidence, not just of our love, but of the times I had failed him, the moments I wished I could take back.

I imagined JR was en route to Heaven, and in a waiting room between here and there, where they process your living paperwork into your past life paperwork, he might get the urge to reread his text messages. I needed to ensure that what he read was the real version of us, not the angry, frustrated, or dismissive version. I couldn't have him entering Heaven without knowing in his heart that we were soulmates and everything was still perfect. I didn't want JR to think anything was ever wrong between us.

With trembling hands, I unlocked my phone and scrolled through the text messages between us. It was like opening a time capsule, each message a snapshot of a life that felt both familiar and impossibly distant. But instead of finding comfort in these memories, I was consumed by a growing dread. I wasn't just reading our love story; I was reliving every argument, every moment of frustration, and every careless word I had ever typed.

The panic tightened its grip on me. I couldn't let these words stand. I couldn't let the world—or JR, wherever he was—remember us like this. I needed to erase the evidence, rewrite the narrative, and ensure that what remained was only love, only the best of us.

I started deleting, my fingers racing across the screen. Scroll, read, delete. Scroll, read, delete. The process was mechanical, almost automatic, but each deletion felt like a small act of redemption. I was trying to cleanse our past, purify it, and make it worthy of our love. At some point, I paused and realized I was about to delete a message about JR forgetting to buy milk. "No," I thought, "the world doesn't need to know that even a soulmate can forget the basics." But then I laughed. JR would've found that hilarious—he'd say even Heaven needs a good grocery list.

But as I continued, I noticed something that stopped me. The messages I was deleting on my phone were often sharp and curt, born out of frustration or exhaustion.

"Fuck you, JR. Then you handle it."

"You aren't listening."

"I don't care."

Once I had gone far enough in my phone and left only a trail of kissing face emojis and love messages with the occasional "Baby, can you grab my…" text, I moved on to his phone.

But when I switched to JR's phone, the story was different. His messages were filled with love, patience, and everyday sweetness that I had taken for granted. There were countless messages in which he checked in on me, made small jokes to lighten my mood, and simply said, "I love you."

Tears welled up in my eyes as I scrolled through his messages, realizing how many of these moments I had overlooked, how many times I had been too busy or too distracted to fully appreciate what he was offering. His phone was full of real snapshots of our lives, the ones that told the true story of us—messy, unfiltered, full of love even amid our imperfections.

A photo he had taken of me laughing with my mouth wide open, hair in disarray, caught my eye. I remembered that moment—not the photo itself, but the laugh, the warmth of his presence as he teased me about something trivial. It was a candid shot, far from the carefully curated images I usually allowed of myself. But it was real. And there were hundreds more like it—pictures of the grandkids, some blurry, some out of focus, but all capturing the essence of our chaotic, wonderful life.

I sank down onto the edge of the bed, clenching both phones to my chest as the tears began to fall freely. In trying to erase the evidence of our imperfections, I had almost erased the evidence of our love—our real love. The kind that survives the arguments, the misunderstandings, the everyday messiness of life. The kind that isn't always pretty but is always true.

I realized then that I didn't need to delete anything. The love JR and I had wasn't perfect, but it was ours. It was real, and it was enough. He knew that, and somewhere deep down, I knew it too.

Slowly, I put both phones down on the bed beside me. I took a deep breath, letting the wave of emotions wash over me.

I didn't need to rewrite our story. I just needed to remember it, to hold on to it, to cherish it—all of it, the good, the bad, and everything in between. I let myself feel the full weight of our life together—the love that had filled our days, the loss that now filled my heart—and realized that I didn't need to hide from the truth. I just needed to carry it with me, to keep it alive in my heart, just as JR would have wanted.

Celebrating JR's Life

In September, we had a celebration of life for JR. It was a beautiful event in our backyard, surrounded by business leaders—about one thousand of our top people. It had to be invite-only; there was no way to invite everyone. We had drones flying overhead, spelling out his famous sayings: "I believe in you," and "Keep growing."

I had turned our backyard into a shrine to his work. We brought in the props he used on stage at our biggest events—everything that he had used over the years to connect to people—to inspire them. I even had an 18-wheeler drive it all from our corporate office in Greensboro. The spaceship, the tightrope, the hamster wheel—everything was there, just like he would have demonstrated on stage.

For the first time, people could step inside the spaceship and walk on the hamster wheel, with some help. Everyone in the Greensboro office thought I was crazy for moving it all to Connecticut, but I didn't care. I needed him to know that nothing he did went unnoticed, that everything he built mattered—to me, and to the people who knew him.

Now, when I look out at my backyard, that's all I see—his presence, his legacy, filling the space.

The October life celebration was equally as touching and moving. I was so overwhelmed with grief, and I wanted JR's celebration of life in Miami to be perfect. But I couldn't get my head screwed on right. So, Alicia Keys offered to plan and organize the celebration in Miami with Amber. From start to finish they handled everything, and it was such a beautiful event, filled with so many touching and magical moments that I know JR would be proud.

Everyone came together to honor and celebrate his life. Jennifer Lopez opened the celebration by giving a moving and heartfelt speech about the impact JR had on her life and their special relationship. Several of our other close friends, like Jamie Foxx, DJ Khaled, Fat Joe, Swizz Beats, Ben Affleck, Alejandro, La La, and Ja Rule took the stage to tell stories and special moments that they shared with JR. The night was capped off by a musical rendition of "Empire State of Mind" with a stage full of talent that would rival the red carpet at the Grammys.

Utopia IV: Docked Grief

A few weeks after returning from Croatia, Marc convinced me to move to *Utopia IV* in New York City for both a change of scenery and as a strategic move to be closer to Amber and the kids.

The *Utopia IV* was big enough for us to live on, so moving there temporarily to be closer to the kids made sense, rather than driving through New York traffic almost daily. Amber's apartment was conveniently located across the street from the boat, which added to the practicality of Marc's idea. It didn't get past me that Marc also would be able to sleep at his own apartment down the street from the boat dock at Chelsea Piers instead of driving back and forth to babysit me in Greenwich.

Returning to the *Utopia IV* for the first time since JR's passing was like reopening an old wound. The *Utopia IV* didn't go out; it stayed docked the entire time. We weren't there to relax or escape. We had just moved our mourning group to a different location. We continued to work from the boat, anchoring ourselves in a place that felt both comforting and practical. The days were filled with grief and a flurry of visitors who came to offer their condolences. People came to visit Amber and me during those weeks of our mourning. Lawyers came to have me sign papers, which thank God for Marc, who went through every legal paper and ensured I knew what I was signing. I was still caught up in the "we should have had more time" mourning period.

During this period, La La Anthony and Serena Williams visited me for the first time since JR's passing. La La had come to Greenwich first and stayed with me during the first celebration of life. She spent the night there, providing much-needed support, and helped us move to the boat. The next day, after we moved to New York, Serena visited us on the boat. We were all very emotional. The atmosphere was far from a sunny escape; we hid in the dark, enveloped in our grief. These visits were not about basking in sunlight or taking leisurely boat rides. Instead, they were about facing our collective grief head-on, supporting one another through our darkest times.

Amber had a hard time. One night, she pulled her clavicle muscle while she slept and couldn't turn her head. I called a therapist to come and work on her neck, which was a small reminder of how life continued to throw challenges our way, no matter what we were dealing with already.

Amber was in significant pain. As the therapist worked on her, I watched as if my vigilance would help her get out of pain faster.

She was talking about how much pain her neck was in, and suddenly, it all came rushing back to me—something I thought I had forgotten. He didn't want a massage that day. I remember telling him, "Relax, have a massage, it'll feel so good." He refused. "I don't want one," he said, frustrated, and I kept pushing. "You should. You'll feel better." Finally, he gave in, almost annoyed. I didn't understand why he was so resistant, or why I was so insistent. It was such a strange moment.

Then it hit me like a ton of bricks: I had pushed him to have that massage. And now, all I could think was, *Why didn't I just let him relax?*

My mouth opened, and words out of order came falling out while Serena tried to catch them like tennis balls flying at her.

I grabbed my computer and Serena said, "Don't do that to yourself. Don't look that up."

The words fell out desperately.

"I was worried about his knee."

"I thought a massage might help relax him."

"I was worried about his knee."

"I thought a massage might help relax him. His knee was giving him so much trouble."

My voice trembling. "Serena, he refused. He said no a few times."

My words flew out in a chaotic rush. "I didn't listen."

"I thought he was being stubborn."

"Why go on vacation with a stiff knee?"

"I pestered him. Nagged him."

"I ordered the massage. I bullied him into getting it."

"What if I…the massage…fuck, fuck, fuck."

I choked out, the realization crashing down like a tidal wave.

Serena was sitting next to me now. Amber had stopped her massage, and the masseuse had disappeared. Amber didn't come closer; she was still processing that this was the first time she had heard about the massage.

"Loren, please don't do this." Serena's voice was firm yet pleading as she saw me reach for my iPad. "Loren? Loren. Don't do this to yourself. You couldn't have known. You don't know. You won't know. Loren."

I grabbed the iPad, punched in my code, and began Googling.

"There was nothing you could do," Serena repeated, like many others had said. She was as close to JR and me as any family member. She was no stranger to PE. Her first experience with a pulmonary embolism was in 2011, which led to hospitalization and significant health concerns. Later, in 2017, after giving birth to her daughter, Olympia, she suffered another pulmonary embolism. This occurred shortly after her emergency C-section, complicating her recovery and leading to further medical interventions, including a filter to prevent additional clots from reaching her lungs. She was a survivor of PE and yet I couldn't accept her authority on the matter. Or I didn't want to. We had spoken practically every day since JR died. She had advice, words of wisdom, and sometimes just an ear to listen to me cry. Her voice soothed me, especially during our late-night calls, but even so, in my tornado of grief, it was hard to hear her completely when she told me it wasn't my fault.

"Loren, you understand the chances of you being able to know that he had a blood clot were pretty slim. And even so, you wouldn't have been able to fix it."

I couldn't stop Googling for different answers.

JR had a background in biology. He was our family's resident doctor, correctly diagnosing poison ivy, sprained wrists, or a lump in your breast. How did he miss this?

I simply could not reconcile it. How could I have not known there was a blood clot? I had a blood clot myself—in 2015, I had a brain aneurysm. I felt it come on while I was at work. I'll never forget how my hands turned gray like I had covered them in newsprint. I felt an electrical shock in my jaw, like an electric current zapped my mouth. After multiple MRIs, tests, scans, and finally, an MRA, which looks at the vessels of the brain versus any masses or tumors in the muscles, I found out I had a massive aneurysm in the back of the center of my brain. Most doctors didn't want to touch it. They said it was going to be too hard to get to it—that I'd probably die during surgery or have a stroke.

But we found the best neurosurgeon, Dr. Aman Patel, through my friends La La Anthony and Carmelo Anthony. Dr. Patel was an expert at endovascular endoscopic operations on the brain, which involved an incision through the veins in the groin. Back then it was still experimental. Though it was a shot in the dark, the surgery succeeded. I had coils and a stent put in place to block the aneurysm, and since my surgery, I have thankfully gotten a clean bill of health. And now, as JR called it, I also have a "blinged-out brain."

JR and I were so on top of our health, especially given the various ailments I've suffered and my parents' health history; there's no way we would have missed something like that. Had we known, we could have had it taken care of. We were two days away from Madrid…seeing the doctor in Spain. Why didn't God give us forty-eight hours more to try and fix the problem in his knee? Why?

I recalled a conversation that Christian and I had over two dozen times last week.

"WHAT THE FUCK! WE WERE DAYS AWAY FROM FIXING THE FUCKING KNEE," I screamed, the frustration and anger boiling over. "THAT'S WHY IT WAS GETTING STIFFER OVER THE LAST FEW WEEKS. THERE WAS A BLOOD CLOT."

The heat rose in my face as I continued, "That's why his blood test was off, and it was also a few weeks after he got the second COVID booster. They now say it has caused clots in some people." I paused, catching my breath.

Always calm and rational, Christian interjected, "And his existing knee problem hid the clot from us."

I nodded, feeling the weight of guilt pressing down on me. "And because of that, we all feel even more guilty."

I repeatedly asked Christian, after returning to the USA, "Was JR acting different backstage? Did JR complain about the knee? What did he say? Was he in pain?" I tortured myself over and over. "How the fuck did we miss this?"

Christian sighed, heavy with shared sorrow.

"How was he on stage? Backstage? Did he complain? Was he different?" I persisted.

"Loren, he was on cloud nine the whole fucking event. It's one of the things that gives me peace." Christian was in the ocean of despair with me but treading water.

"Yep," I agreed, still flailing. "None of it makes fucking sense. It makes no sense. He was happy. Healthy. Fuck. One time in his life, his blood was off," I continued. "His platelets were not on the normal side. The doctors said it was probably an error or mistake and that we would repeat it. The only time his blood work wasn't perfect..."

"Loren," Christian rarely interrupted me. "We've had this conversation at least twenty times. And it never feels any better."

I drifted back to the next day after they had taken JR off the boat. I was bombarding the coroner with questions.

"The breath you saw him take was his last breath," the coroner said. "He was holding his breath. I'm sure he was scared for a second. But that was his last breath."

The coroner's office in Croatia was so certain JR had suffered a pulmonary embolism that they didn't recommend an autopsy. Both the Croatian and Greenwich funeral directors noted signs supporting this, including details of how they found his body.

"He never made it to the bed," the coroner said. "If he were waiting for you, he would have been on the bed, not the floor. Why would he have sat on the floor? No, he fell on the floor. He would have sat on the bed if he had been waiting for you. Then he would have passed out backward on the bed." This exact conversation I reenacted over and over again for months.

I had heard that when some people die, there is a moment just before they are gone when they can hear a relative say, "I'm not ready for you to go yet." And in hearing those words, somehow the dying person is able to come back, revived by the loving and pleading. I often wondered if I had missed the chance to say those words and if JR might have come back from death had I known to say the words.

Torturing myself. Aware that I was torturing myself and continuing to do it. In some way, inflicting pain on myself was fine because I felt like I deserved it.

You hear stories of people dying who couldn't talk in those final moments, or they say they have to sit down or they feel weak. Or they yell, "I'm not ready!" I had never experienced death like this before. Both of my parents had passed away already, my mother early on. So I was familiar with death…but never like this…I have been with JR longer than anyone in my life. This felt like an amputation.

There is nothing ordinary about losing your everything.

Forgiving the Unforgivable

"There was nothing you could do, Loren." I could feel my forehead soften a bit as the thoughts continued to run through my head, churning as if on a hamster wheel.

Then, Serena asked me something that instantly stopped the wheel and that I'd never forget.

"What would you have done if your daughter had been there?" she asked me. "What if she said to you, 'Mom, I couldn't face that. I couldn't see Dad like that. I didn't want to see his face in that situation. I wanted to remember him the way we were.' Would you be mad at Amber?"

"No, of course not, I would understand completely," I responded quickly. "I would have loved my daughter twice as hard, Serena."

I would have held her, consoled her, told her anything to relieve whatever pain she felt.

"Then why can't you forgive yourself?" Serena said, releasing it into the sea air. It took flight like a seagull soaring silently above us.

In that moment, a tiny light broke through the dark clouds of my grief. Looking at my actions through the lens of another person, my daughter, someone I had unconditional love for, helped me show myself the grace I would have given her. I had to accept that there's no typical response to seeing your husband dead on the floor. I let out a deep breath. I said only loud enough for me to hear: "He forgives you, Loren, and he loves you."

Echoes of His Presence

Days blurred together, a haze of grief and disbelief that turned minutes into hours, hours into days. Time became a concept that had lost its meaning. I was adrift in a sea of sorrow, the sharp edges of reality dulled by the overwhelming weight of loss. Yet, amidst the fog, there were anchors—small, tangible things that kept me tethered to the memory of JR. His belongings were scattered throughout our home in Greenwich, remnants of a life we had shared, now eerily still in his absence.

Returning to Greenwich was like walking into a different world. The house, once filled with his laughter, the hum of daily life, now stood silent. The stillness pressed down on me, a suffocating weight that grew heavier with every step I took. The familiar surroundings seemed foreign, as if the walls were grieving, mourning the man who had once filled every corner with his vibrant energy.

Amid this silence, panic set in—a deep, primal fear that gnawed at the edges of my sanity. The thought was unbearable, and I felt a surge of desperation take hold.

Without thinking, I began to move through the house with a frantic urgency, my heart pounding. I tore through our closet, pulling out the clothes he had worn on our trip to Croatia, still infused with his scent. That scent—earthy, warm, uniquely JR—was my lifeline, my last tangible connection to him. I held his shirt close to my face, inhaling deeply, letting the scent fill my lungs, trying to capture it, to hold on to it as if it were something I could keep forever.

But I knew it wouldn't last. Scents fade, just as memories do. And the thought of losing that, of losing him again in some small way, was more than I could bear.

I grabbed a stack of large Ziploc bags from the kitchen and began methodically sealing his clothes. Each piece was handled with reverence as if it were a sacred artifact. His favorite tracksuit, the one he wore when we relaxed in the evenings, his hat, still holding the shape of his head, his T-shirts, soft from countless washes—all were carefully folded and zipped into the plastic bags. The sound of the zipper closing felt like a finality I wasn't ready to accept, but I pressed on, sealing each bag with the determination of someone trying to preserve their soul.

I plastered the bags with notes written in bold, desperate letters: "Do not touch." It was as if writing the words could command time to stand still, to stop the inevitable fading of his scent. The bags were my way of holding onto him, of keeping him close in a world that felt increasingly distant.

But as the days turned into weeks, the scent began to fade. The airtight seals couldn't stop time; with each passing day, he slipped further away, and the panic that once drove me to preserve his essence turned into crushing despair.

The Scent of Memory

One day, in desperation, I ventured into his bathroom. The room was a sanctuary, still filled with the small, everyday items that had been part of his routine. His toothbrush, razor, and aftershave were all untouched since the day he left. And there it was, sitting on the counter as if waiting for me—his cologne.

JR had only worn two colognes; both were favorites I could identify anywhere. The Bulgari bottle caught my eye first, the

familiar black and silver label set against the black marble coun-
tertop. My hands trembled as I reached for it, the cool glass
smooth under my fingers. I held the bottle close, staring at it
like a relic from another life.

With a deep breath, I pressed the nozzle, and the room was
instantly filled with his rich, warm, intoxicating scent. It was as
if he had walked into the room, wrapping me in his presence
and flooding me with memories. I closed my eyes, letting the
scent envelop me, and for the first time in what felt like forever,
I could breathe.

In a frenzy, I began spraying the cologne everywhere—on
my clothes, in the air, even on the furniture. The scent clung
to the fabric and to my skin, filling the space around me with
the essence of JR. It was a desperate act, a way to reclaim some
part of him that I had feared was lost forever. As the fragrance
wrapped around me, I felt a bittersweet happiness that was
almost too much to bear.

But it wasn't just me who needed that connection. With his
innocent, wide-eyed curiosity, Ayden had been watching me,
his slight figure standing in the doorway, unsure of what to do.
Without thinking, I turned to him, holding out the bottle of
cologne as if offering him a piece of his Pop Pop. "Come here,
baby," I whispered, my voice thick with emotion. "Let's put
some on you too."

He stepped forward, his eyes searching mine, and I sprayed
the cologne onto his little shirt and arms. The scent clung to
him, mixing with childhood's sweet, familiar smell. He looked
up at me, and I saw a flicker of recognition in his eyes—a connection to the man he had loved so deeply and lost so suddenly.

Ayden wrapped his small arms around my legs, his grip
surprisingly strong for someone so young. In that embrace, I

felt the shift—a quiet, shared understanding that connected us more deeply than words ever could. He cared for me as much as I cared for him, his presence grounding me in a way I hadn't expected. We stood there, wrapped in JR's scent, sharing our grief in the only way we knew how.

A tear slipped down my cheek, and Ayden reached up to wipe it away, his touch gentle and comforting. We both smiled, our faces reflecting the bittersweet mixture of love and loss that hung in the air. We missed him together, and we found a small measure of peace in that shared sorrow.

Breaking the Surface

As I started to reemerge from my depths of mourning, I began to venture out of my protective refuge. Each small step felt like testing the waters for threats, but I realized I couldn't let my fear, my deep need to punish myself, keep punishing others. Just as I had to push beyond my protective barriers, I had to allow myself to experience life again.

One evening, as the sun dipped low and cast a warm, golden hue across the living room, I sat with Amber and the grandkids, trying to stitch together some semblance of normalcy. The air was thick with the usual sounds of a family settling into the evening—a distant television, the clatter of dishes in the kitchen, and the soft murmur of conversation. But beneath it all was an unspoken weight, a lingering sadness that clung to us like the fading light of day.

Ayden, ever the curious and playful spirit, had discovered an old toy frog that had somehow survived the chaos of recent months. It was one of those silly toys that, when pressed just right, emitted a surprisingly realistic croak. His tiny fingers worked the mechanism with practiced ease, and soon the room was filled with the peculiar, almost absurd sound of a frog's croak. Ayva, never one to be outdone by her older brother, quickly joined in, her tiny voice mimicking the frog with a surprising accuracy that made us all pause.

Their combined efforts soon turned the living room into a cacophony of croaks—loud, erratic, and entirely out of place in our otherwise subdued evening. The sheer ridiculousness of it all—two little kids pretending to be frogs during our heavy grief—was so outlandish and unexpected that it caught me off guard.

And then it happened.

A laugh—small at first, barely more than a breath—escaped my lips. It was as if my body was unsure if it was still capable of such an act. But that laugh grew as Ayden and Ayva continued their amphibian antics, jumping around the room with exaggerated hops and croaks. And then Aydrien joined in. Now there were three frogs in the living room. It bubbled up deep within me, rising like a long-submerged buoy, finally breaking the surface.

It was a laugh I hadn't felt in what seemed like a lifetime—pure, unfiltered, and entirely uncontrollable. It filled the room, mingling with the children's croaks, creating a symphony of absurdity that chased away the shadows clinging to my heart. The weight of grief lifted momentarily, and I was just Mimi, laughing with her grandchildren, lost in a moment of pure, unadulterated joy. And in that moment, I realized with startling clarity that it was possible to feel this way again. Even in the depths of my sorrow, life still could surprise me with its capacity for joy.

Easter Without the Eggs

As time passed, the holidays came and went, each bringing a fresh wave of heartache and new opportunities for connection and laughter. I spent more and more time with the grandkids, their boundless energy and innocent view of the world acting as a balm to my wounded soul.

When Easter approached, I suggested to Amber taking the kids away for a break, a chance to escape the memories that clung to our home like old cobwebs. I knew the legendary Easter egg hunt was not going to be the same this year.

But I couldn't bear letting the holiday pass without acknowledgment or some small act connecting us to the past. "Go and enjoy," I told her, "but we'll celebrate when you return."

I wasn't prepared for the brutal task of setting up the Easter egg hunt. We always did them at the Miami house. It had these magnificent gardens. JR would orchestrate legendary Easter egg hunts for our grandkids and their friends. JR had a knack for making these hunts unforgettable. He had eggs with candy, others with toys. He would get one hundred golden eggs filled with money, far more exciting than the regular-colored ones. Some eggs contained $1, $10, $20, $50, and even $100 wrapped in aluminum foil. JR would hide the eggs himself, often forgetting where he put them, much to everyone's amusement.

This year, we authorized significant renovations of the whole house, including the teardown of the gardens, and we were looking for more bedrooms so the grandkids could visit—which we now didn't need. April 2022 marked our last Easter egg hunt before the renovation. Once alive and brimming with trees, green hedges, and flower bushes, the lush gardens were replaced by construction and new walls. The absence of the gardens mirrored the void JR's passing had left in my heart.

Confused yet purposeful, I set up the Easter egg hunt in the Miami condo I was staying at while renovations were completed. I walked around the new space and hid the eggs, all one hundred of them. Each hidden egg was a small act of defiance against the crushing weight of loss, a fragile thread connecting the past to the present, helping me navigate through the painful waters of healing. As I placed each egg, I could almost hear JR's voice, reminding me to make the hunt challenging, to hide them well.

As I finished placing the last egg in its hiding spot, I felt a slight sense of accomplishment, as if I had honored JR's memory in some small yet significant way.

Love's Quiet Persistence

As I spent more time with the grandkids, I smiled more. I listened to their laughter, jokes, and observations; their little voices were more precise the more present I tried to be with them. The small moments with them got me through my inner isolation—moments like when FaceTime popped up on my phone and Ayden was smiling at me.

"Hi, baby," I said.

"Mimi," he squealed. "Look! We've got a turtle!"

"That's great, baby!" My eyes widened at this smiling boy on FaceTime holding up a baby turtle.

About this time, I began to feel a shift between myself and my grandbabies. It was before I left for a trip to Paris. It was my first outing with my friend Jennifer and my first girls' trip. A few days before I left, the kids came to the house.

I put out all of their favorite games like I used to. We went swimming and played "Sharks in the Pool," something that they would play weekly with JR. He wore a fin on his back, they would throw foam noodles at him, and he loved it! We played competitive rounds of Uno, the boys hollering every time they made me Draw Four. We played crystal art games on our computers, ate snacks, and laughed at silly videos on YouTube. The time flew by. My cheeks were flushed from the activity—I had not run around with my grandkids like this in months. It felt good to get my heart pumping from child's play again.

As nightfall taunted us, they rushed over to me. "Can you come over again before you leave for Paris so we can continue playing?"

When JR was alive, they always asked JR for more time. "Can we do this again? Can you come over, Mimi and Pop Pop?" But they hadn't asked me for anything in months. They knew I hadn't been me. They knew I wasn't happy. Children have more intuition than we realize.

"Yes," I said. No excuses, no work, no hiding. "Yes."

They gathered around me, hugging me with tight grips. "This feels like the days used to be with Pop Pop," I heard Ayva say.

And Aydrien, my youngest and arguably most intuitive, looked up at me. "I miss Pop Pop."

"Me too," I told him, hugging him tight and smiling, "but he'd be happy playing together today. He'd smile that we were having such a good day and that you beat me in paddle-ball and Uno."

"Yep!" Aydrien responded and broke out into a little happy dance shaking his arms and wiggling his butt as he would usually do when he would beat JR in anything.

Kids aren't supposed to fill our cups, but my cup runneth over with joy that day. I smiled long after the toys were put away and the house was clean. I put my hand on my heart as I went to bed, inspecting that hole again. I could have sworn it shrunk in size just a little. I knew for sure it hurt a little less that night. I closed my eyes, comforted that the kids felt their Mimi was back with them.

The Lesson: Grief is Not All Bad

Grief doesn't diminish love; it sharpens its presence, etching it into our souls with a clarity we couldn't perceive before. In the aftermath of loss, love lingers not just in the possessions we cling to or the rituals we repeat, but in the quiet, unexpected moments that catch us off guard—a shared laugh with grandchildren, the scent that fills a room, the memories that resurface without warning. These are not mere reminders of what was, but affirmations of what still is.

JR's presence isn't something I need to hold on to physically; it's woven into the very fabric of my life, continually shaping who I am. His voice may no longer be audible, but his lessons, his values, and his love resonate louder than ever, guiding my decisions and nurturing my spirit.

Moving forward isn't about letting go; it's about embracing the transformation of love as it persists in new forms. It's about recognizing that love evolves, just as we do, and learning to accept its presence in places we never expected to find it. Love becomes a compass, quietly guiding me through even the darkest days, reminding me that the strength to carry on is rooted in the love that was shared.

Grief may be heavy, but it's love that gives it substance—and it's love that ultimately lightens the load, allowing me to carry on with a renewed sense of purpose. Love doesn't fade with time; it deepens, creating a well of resilience and grace that we draw from, day after day. This is the love that sustains us, the love that endures beyond loss, and the love that propels us forward, even when the road ahead seems uncertain.

In this journey, I've learned that love is not just a memory—it's a living, breathing force that continues to shape our lives. It is the thread that ties our past to our future, allowing us to honor what was while embracing what is yet to come. By allowing love to guide us, we find the strength to transform grief into growth, and loss into legacy.

CHAPTER FIVE

ANGER, ANGUISH, AND APOLOGIES

GRIEF DOESN'T JUST CREEP IN; it settles like an unwelcome guest, anchoring itself in every quiet corner of your life, transforming the most mundane moments into unbearable reminders of absence. It's not simply that you're weighed down by it—grief becomes the air around you, heavy, oppressive, until each breath feels like a struggle. After JR died, it wasn't a matter of feeling consumed; I was flattened by it and slammed to the ground, left gasping. Each attempt to rise felt futile, as though any movement might summon grief's swift return, pinning me down again and pressing me deeper into the floor. And even when I managed to get up, I never truly stood. I stayed half-crouched, braced for the next strike. Loneliness, guilt, anger, regret—grief's many accomplices—circling, waiting for the right moment to knock me back down. People tell you to move on, to keep going, but they don't understand that for me, standing still is survival. Losing JR was so profound, so all-consuming. When I lost JR, it was like being in a room filled with people…but I couldn't see or hear any of them. I was alone and broken. It was an attempt to fix the broken part that led me to therapy.

The Advice of Strangers

I walked into the therapist's office, a part of me already regretting the decision. The walls were painted in soft, neutral tones, designed to be calming, I'm sure, but instead, they made me feel trapped in some sort of beige purgatory. The air was heavy with the scent of lavender—too much lavender—like the kind you'd find in an overzealous yoga studio.

The therapist was waiting for me with that same serene smile she always had, the kind that made me want to slap it right off her face some days. Today was one of those days. I sat across from her, trying to get comfortable on the overly plush couch that seemed to swallow me whole. As usual, she offered me tea, and I declined. I wasn't here for tea.

"So, Loren," she began, her voice soft, almost a whisper, like she was afraid to disturb the grief that clung to me like a second skin. "How are you feeling today?"

I stared at her for a moment, contemplating whether I should tell her the truth—but instead, I gave her the answer she wanted. "I'm fine."

She nodded as if she understood, but how could she? She didn't know him. She didn't know us. But she acted like she did, and that was almost worse.

"I've been thinking," she said, leaning forward slightly, her hands folded neatly in her lap. "You've made a lot of progress in dealing with your situation, Loren. You've been incredibly strong."

I didn't feel strong. I felt I barely held on most days, but I didn't say that. I just waited, knowing there was more coming. There was always more.

"But," she continued, "I think it might be time to start considering your future."

"My future?" I echoed, not entirely sure where she was going with this.

"Yes," she said, her smile widening just a fraction. "I know it might seem too soon, but...."

I blinked at her, trying to process what she was saying. But?

"Maybe it's time to consider dating again, Loren," she said, her voice laced with that practiced gentleness therapists are taught in school, the kind that always seems to carry a hint of condescension, as if I were a child being coaxed into a conversation I wasn't ready for.

I stared at her, the words hanging like a bad joke that wasn't funny the first time. Dating? Again? The very thought sent a cold wave of disbelief washing over me. JR had been gone for—what, four months? Maybe five? Time had blurred into a haze of sleepless nights and endless days, each one bleeding into the next. Sitting across from me in her overly lavender-smelling office, this woman told me to move on, as if JR were just some phase I'd gone through—a chapter to close before flipping to the next.

The absurdity of it was almost laughable. Almost. But instead of laughing, I was pissed. Furious. I felt the weight of her suggestion pressing down on me, pushing me closer to being flat out on the ground. "Move on," she had said, as if that were even possible. As if I could just replace him with another man like swapping out a broken appliance.

I didn't respond. What was there to say? My mind was a storm of conflicting emotions—anger, disbelief, hopelessness, despair, and apathy that settled in my chest like a lead weight. I stood up, the suddenness of the movement surprising even me. My bag was already in my hand, though I didn't remember picking it up.

"I think we're done here," I heard myself say, my voice flat, detached, as though it belonged to someone else. The therapist—what was her name again? It didn't matter—she started to say something, her voice rising slightly in a plea to stay, to talk it out, but I was already halfway to the door. I didn't look back.

The hallway outside her office felt cold and unwelcoming as I made my way to the elevator. My heels clicking against the polished floor echoed in the empty corridor, a harsh contrast to the suffocating silence that had settled over me like a shroud. I pressed the elevator button with more force than necessary, willing the doors to open, to take me away from this place, this absurd suggestion that I could ever "move on."

Back in the car, I sat for a moment, staring at the steering wheel, my mind replaying the conversation in an endless loop. The idea of dating again was so foreign, so utterly disconnected from the reality I was living in that I couldn't even entertain it. How could I? JR wasn't just my husband—he was my human— the only one who ever—would ever—truly understand me in all my complexities and contradictions. The idea of finding that with someone else was not just impossible; it was a betrayal of everything we had built together.

I started the car, the engine's hum a dull background noise to the storm raging inside me. As I drove home, I felt a dark humor bubbling up inside me, a bitter irony that made me want to laugh and cry simultaneously—moving on? What kind of advice was I paying for?

The house was quiet when I walked in, the quiet that only exists when a place has been emptied of its soul. And I realized, with a comforting and devastating clarity, that I wasn't ready to let any of it go. Not yet.

Not ever.

Hurting and Hurting Those You Love

The kitchen was too quiet, almost suffocating in its stillness. The only sound came from the apple I was chewing, each bite feeling like a small defiance against the emptiness around me. Then it happened.

"Mom, I've arranged a schedule," Amber said, stepping into the kitchen, her hands fidgeting with her phone, the list of names and times glowing on the screen. "Mary's staying over tomorrow night, Christian's the day after that, then Natalia on Friday…I don't want you to be alone. You know, just in case."

I looked up from the apple, unsure I was hearing her right. "A schedule?" The words tasted bitter in my mouth. "You're scheduling people to babysit me now?"

Amber hesitated. Her eyes were soft, full of concern, like she was afraid to say the wrong thing. "It's just…since the kids and I can't always be here, I wanted to ensure someone is. I don't want you alone, Mom. Not yet."

I felt something hot rising in me—rage, resentment, humiliation. The apple in my hand suddenly felt like a weapon, something I wanted to throw across the room, something I could crush in my palm. "I don't need a damn babysitter," I spat, my voice sharper than I intended. "I'm not a child. I'm not some fragile egg that's going to crack."

"Mom…" Amber's voice wavered, but she pressed on, trying to maintain the calm, steady tone she'd used ever since JR died. "It's not that. I just—" she paused, searching for the right words. "I remember how you were after Dad passed. You weren't sleeping. You barely ate. I was scared—am *still* scared—that you might…I don't know…"

"Do something?" I snapped, my eyes narrowing. "Like what, Amber? You think I'm going to hurt myself? Is that it?"

Amber's face fell, her shoulders slumping as she sighed. "I don't know, Mom. I don't know what you're capable of right now. You haven't been the same. You fired your therapist—again. That's five therapists now. Maybe it's time to try another one? A sixth one?"

The audacity of her words hit me like a slap. I stood up from the counter, the chair scraping against the floor with a grating screech. "I don't need another damn therapist, Amber!" I shouted. "I don't need you, or Mary, or Christian, or *Natalia* coming in here and watching me like I'm some toddler. I don't need you deciding what's best for me."

The silence after my outburst was deafening. Amber didn't move. She didn't argue. She just stood there, staring at me with those wide, green eyes—the same eyes that JR used to look at me with whenever I lost control.

As I gripped the counter, my mind raced back to those agonizing days on the ship after JR had passed. Amber wasn't with me in Croatia, and I could still feel the weight of her worry, her fear stretching across continents. I hadn't realized it then—how could I, drowning in my grief?—but she was frantic. She was terrified that I wouldn't survive without JR. Amber had begged

Marc to check on me constantly, fearing that I might do something reckless—overdose on the sleeping pills the doctors had prescribed, or worse. She knew, better than anyone, how close her father and I had been and how intertwined our lives were. The idea of me existing without him was something she couldn't bear, and so she clung to the only thing she had left—protecting me, even from herself.

Amber had always been strong, but in those moments, I hadn't realized just how much she had taken on. Amber had told me, again and again, that she was mourning both of us. When JR died, she said, I died too—at least the part of me she knew. I wasn't the same anymore. I wanted to disagree, to argue that I was still here, but I couldn't. She'd been through her version of hell, and I wasn't there for her. She lost her father, and in some ways, she lost the mother she knew too. I was a different version of Loren now. Maybe she was right. Maybe we'll never be who we were.

Marc had told me how, when I was on the boat in Croatia after JR died, Amber would whisper into the phone, her voice cracking with panic, begging him to stand outside my door while I showered, just in case. She didn't trust that I would make it through the night without him. I had never felt more loved and, at the same time, more suffocated.

And now, standing here in this kitchen, with Amber watching me as if I might crumble at any moment, I could see the toll it had taken on her. The sleepless nights, the endless worry, the way she had pushed her own grief aside to care for me. But even now, I couldn't let her in. I couldn't let her take on my pain on top of her own.

"I'm sorry you feel that way," Amber said quietly, her voice barely above a whisper. "But I'm still doing it. They're still coming over, even if you don't like it."

Her words only fueled my anger. With a thud, I threw the apple into the sink, gripping the counter as if I might break it in half. "Do whatever the hell you want. Clearly, you already have."

Amber nodded slowly, her face still heartbreakingly calm, like she'd resigned herself to my fury. "I know you don't want this, Mom. But you're not the only one who lost Dad. And I can't lose you too."

And there it was—the weight of it, the fear that she had been carrying all this time. It was in her eyes, in her voice. She was terrified. Not just of losing JR, but of losing me too. And in my grief, I had been so consumed by my own pain that I hadn't even realized what I was putting her through.

But even in that moment, even with the guilt threatening to choke me, I couldn't let go of my anger. I couldn't let her take control of my life, not after everything that had been taken from me. So I did what I always did—I pushed her away.

"Fine," I said coldly, turning my back to her. "Do what you have to do. Just leave me alone."

Amber didn't respond. She just stood there for a moment, watching me, before turning and quietly walking out of the kitchen, leaving me alone with my anger, my grief, and the unbearable weight of what I had just done.

She was trying to help me, trying to take care of me, but all I could see was the way she was treating me like a fragile thing, something that might break at any moment. And in that moment, I saw that I had spent my entire life showing her what it was like to be a strong woman, until now.

85

Amber—my beautiful, responsible daughter—was just caught in the crossfire of loss.

Grieving Together, Finally

The mattresses were scattered across the floor, small islands in a sea of disarray. I sat perched on the bed, the sheets heavy and unmade. Ayden had pulled his mattress closest to me, his small form barely noticeable beneath the blankets. The others—Ayva and Aydrien—were wrapped in their own cocoons of sleep, their soft breaths the only sound in the quiet room.

It was Amber's idea, this nightly ritual of gathering everyone together. I never asked her to explain why. Perhaps she didn't need to; the silence that had settled over our house after JR's death explained it all. It wasn't the sleep we were afraid of. It was what came after.

A sob pierced the silence. Low at first, but enough to catch me. I turned, and Ayden was curled tightly on his side, his small shoulders shaking. His attempt to stay quiet, to hold it in, only made the sound more painful.

I slid off the bed slowly—careful not to disrupt the fragile stillness we had made. Kneeling beside him, I placed a hand on his back, his body trembling beneath my palm.

"Ayden," I whispered, my voice hesitant, unsure. "What is it, baby?"

He rubbed his eyes with the back of his hand, not yet ready to meet my gaze. "I miss Pop Pop," he whispered, his voice catching. "I miss him so much, Mimi."

His words, so simple, hung in the air. The kind of truth that doesn't need embellishment.

It struck me then—how much I had missed, how much I had failed to see. In the weeks after JR passed, I had been consumed, so singularly focused on my grief that the rest of the world became blurred and distant. Even these tiny beings—my grandchildren—had become part of the background noise of my mourning. They had lost their Pop Pop, but they had lost something else too. They had lost me.

I took Ayden into my arms, feeling his weight, his sadness pressing against me. He cried softly into my chest, and I let him. I hadn't realized, until that moment, how much I needed to hold him, to be held by him.

"I'm so sorry," I whispered into his hair, my voice barely audible. The words felt inadequate, too small to capture the vastness of the loss, of the guilt. But they were the only words I had.

Aydrien and Ayva stirred, their sleep broken by their brother's quiet sobs. Without a word, they crawled from their mattresses and over to us, their small bodies pressing against mine, forming a circle of warmth, of grief, of something that felt like love but more fragile.

For a long time, we stayed like that. There was no talking, no need for it. There was just the holding, the being. And in that stillness, I realized something I hadn't allowed myself to feel since JR died—that we were all grieving. And maybe—just maybe—grieving wasn't something you had to do alone.

"I miss him too," I finally said, my voice breaking. "I miss him every day."

The words felt raw, stripped of pretense, as though admitting my grief out loud made it real in a way that was different from the internal weight I had been carrying.

As the minutes passed, the room didn't feel quite as heavy. The grief was still there, but it had softened somehow, the edges no longer as sharp. And in that moment, I understood that maybe being strong wasn't about holding it all in. Maybe it was about letting others hold it with you.

The Space Between Grief and Forgiveness

Amber was sitting at the kitchen table, her hands wrapped around a coffee cup as though holding it together would keep her from falling apart. I approached the table slowly, the weight of what I had to say pressing against my chest. Amber didn't look up, didn't need to. She knew I was there, and maybe she was waiting for this, or perhaps she had long stopped waiting, resigned to the mother I had become.

"Amber," I began, surprised at how rough my voice sounded. "I need to apologize."

I waited for her to turn toward me, but she didn't. The silence was a canyon between us, one that had grown wider in the months since JR's death. I wasn't sure if it could be crossed anymore, but I had to try.

"I'm sorry," I continued, my words stumbling out awkwardly, not because they weren't true but because they had waited too long. "I haven't been there for you. You've been carrying this—carrying me—while I've been drowning in my grief."

I stopped, hoping for some acknowledgment, but Amber stayed quiet. Her face was drawn, her eyes tired. The same eyes JR had, eyes that could see through my defenses. She looked older and wearier. I had missed that before.

"I know you lost him too," I said, forcing the words out. "I should have seen that. I should have been there for you—been your mother. But instead, I left you to hold everything up. And I'm sorry for that."

Amber's eyes finally met mine, full of the quiet pain she had been holding back. For months, she had taken care of me, of the family, of everything that had fallen apart since JR's death while I let her. And now, faced with her pain, my apology felt small, inadequate.

"You've been doing everything," I whispered, my voice trembling now. "And I haven't even asked how you're doing. I should have been the one taking care of you."

There it was: the truth. Not a neat truth, but an ugly, jagged one. Amber had been carrying my burden of grief alongside her own, and I hadn't noticed.

"I'm so sorry," I said again, my voice breaking. "For all of it."

Amber didn't say anything for a moment, but I could see the tears brimming in her eyes. I moved toward her, tentatively, and when I finally placed my arms around her, she didn't pull away. Instead, she leaned into me, and for the first time, I felt the full weight of what she had been holding.

We sat in this delicate space between breaking and mending, because real grief isn't tied up with a neat resolution. It lingers. And so does forgiveness.

Lesson: The Weight We Share

Grief doesn't exist in a vacuum. It's easy to believe, especially when the weight of loss feels unbearable that you're the only one carrying it. You focus so much on your own pain, your own struggle to stand back up, that you miss the people around you, struggling just as much—sometimes even more. I learned this the hard way. I let myself believe that my grief was unique and that no one else could possibly understand what I was going through. But the truth is, Amber was carrying just as much as I was—maybe more.

The people who love us don't just stand by and watch us fall apart. They pick up our pieces, even while they're trying to hold their own together. Amber lost her father, and in so many ways, she lost the mother she knew too. And still, she stayed. Still, she fought to protect me from my own grief, even as she was drowning in her own.

So here's the lesson: grief is not something to be done alone. You don't need to carry it all by yourself and don't need to push away the people trying to help you. Let them in. Let them carry some of the weight with you. It doesn't make the pain any less real but makes it a little more bearable.

If you're grieving, don't forget to look up every once in a while. See who's standing next to you. And if they're carrying a load too—acknowledge it. Help them with it. Grief, as much as it isolates us, can also be the thing that connects us and binds us in our shared experience of love and loss.

Remember, strength doesn't always mean holding it all in. Sometimes it means letting others hold it with you.

CHAPTER SIX

EGGSHELLS AND EXECUTIVE DECISIONS

Time: Five Months AJRD

Old Soul, New Grief

JR WAS AN OLD SOUL—ROMANTIC and old-fashioned. What a combination. A simple way to explain JR's old-fashioned way of connecting with me was when I stepped back and showed some vulnerability, letting him be my man. This was a subtle nuance in our relationship. He never held me back, but during those private times when I would be vulnerable with him and lay my head in his lap, he grew ten feet tall. When I surrendered my strength and allowed myself to be open and tender, it fueled his passion for writing all those heartfelt letters. Looking back, I realize those letters were his way of pouring strength into me, fortifying me for the battles he knew I'd face. Those moments of connection and love mattered most to him, more than anything else. Old-fashioned or not, I fell for it every time.

The Missing Piece

When JR and I slept together, he always insisted on spooning so I could place my heart on the top curvature of his back and feel his heart beating in time with mine. Every night, whether we had just been out to a party or had a big fight, he insisted that we fall asleep with our hearts touching as if we could sync up the beats. It was another one of his love rituals that I took for granted.

Months after Croatia, I began getting out of bed in the morning feeling like my body was missing something. Not metaphorically but physically missing something. It was the oddest feeling. One morning, brushing my teeth, I ran my hand down my stomach and felt what I can only describe as an indentation. It was as if a part of me had been hollowed out. I looked down and saw nothing unusual, but when I touched my stomach, I felt it—a crescent moon shape carved out of my flesh. My fingers could trace its edges. When I mentioned it to a few people, I got the "Oh, she's not thinking clearly" look. So I shut my mouth. But it was there.

For the first few days, I dismissed it as a side effect of lack of sleep, not eating enough, too much stress at work, or just poor old sadness. But the sensation persisted. Grief is tricky like that—it settles into your bones, reshaping you in ways you can't see but you can feel. One night, as I curled into the fetal position, which had become my preferred method of falling asleep, I was acutely aware that my body was missing something. I ran my hand down my belly's flat and felt it—I was concave. My body had a hollow void. I looked down at my stomach and my hips—flat. But as I ran my hand across my hips and over my belly there was the dip, like an inverted moon. I was aware of it but not startled as I drifted to sleep.

The next morning I awoke with a shockwave, grabbing my stomach. It occurred to me that I might be trapped inside a nightmare, feeling my body hollowing out. Then reality hit and I was wide awake, immediately grabbing my pillow and hugging it to my body, hoping to fill the emptiness and squeeze away the loneliness. I clutched that pillow for what seemed like hours, but my heart didn't sync up with another's beat, and that concave feeling wouldn't leave. I couldn't force it to fill, no matter how hard I tried.

Tears don't fill this newly emptied space, and time does not fill it in; I know this now.

Seeing What's Missing

As the days went by, I began to feel—no, I knew—that everyone I encountered could see it too. The curved-in, concave areas on my body that JR used to occupy. They could see the indentation on my hip where JR used to place his hand. They could see the recessed part of my chest where my heart was no longer whole. It was as if grief had carved a map of loss into my muscles, visible to anyone who bothered to look. People on the street, total strangers, would look twice at me, the missing parts of me, the holes and indents in my form, and they would just give me a look of pity. I knew this to be true.

I was positive that perfect strangers were taking two and three glances at me—the woman with permanent curvatures indented into her body where her soulmate used to take up space. I was like a circus freak. Friends and Market America entrepreneurs would see me for the first time since JR died, and they didn't know what to say. So they gave me that look. Shock. Or was it pity and confusion? I hated that look. Their lost expression like their face was in a holding pattern until their brain found the right thing, or anything, to say to me: "Oh my gosh."

What came out of their mouth was even worse: "I'm surprised to see you" or "You look so good despite it all." Like they didn't expect to see me walking upright. I don't have a disease. I just have a broken heart. But that's the thing about grief— people think they have to say something profound when all I want is to be treated normally as if my grief isn't contagious. Can't they just say something kind? Can't they just treat me normally instead of making me feel like I should be quarantined away from the world because I'm grieving? I understand people don't know what to say, but it feels like a slap when people give me that look because they're uncomfortable with my presence. Grief isn't comfortable, but it's also not contagious. Back then I wished they understood that silence is sometimes the best comfort—just being there is enough.

Even at work, where I hoped to find some semblance of normalcy, the same unspoken pity lingered. My team at Market America must have been able to see it too—the indentations in my body—but they knew better than to point out that I wasn't whole. They saw my struggle, but they also saw my determination to carry on JR's legacy. They respected the battle I was fighting, even if they couldn't fully understand it.

Navigating the New Normal

I sat at the kitchen table, the house's quiet pressing down on me. With a deep breath, I sipped my coffee, holding to the warmth like a fall sweater. The silence in the house was deafening, a stark contrast to the constant hum of JR's presence. I picked up my tablet and began scrolling through the morning news, needing to stay informed but also to distract my restless mind.

The headline of one article grabbed my attention: "Amazon to Lay Off 18,000 Employees Amid Economic Uncertainty." I sighed, feeling the weight of the world's economic challenges mirrored in our struggles at Market America. The article detailed how Amazon cut costs due to a drop in post-pandemic sales. It was a reminder that no one is immune to the forces of change— not even giants like Amazon and certainly not Market America. It made me think of our battles with supply chain disruptions and inflation.

Swiping to the following article, I found a piece on Rihanna's pregnancy announcement. "Rihanna's Super Bowl Halftime Performance: Pregnant and Glowing," the headline read. I couldn't help but smile at the photo of Rihanna, looking radiant and powerful. It was a brief moment of joy in an otherwise heavy morning. I admired how she managed to shine and thrive in such a public spotlight, a sentiment I tried to emulate in my public appearances. If she could stand strong under the world's gaze, so could I.

Another notification popped up about the ongoing conflict between Russia and Ukraine. "Germany to Send Leopard 2 Tanks to Ukraine Amid Escalating Tensions," it read. I felt a pang of sorrow for the people caught in the crossfire, their lives upended by forces beyond their control. It reminded me of the unpredictability and fragility of life, something I had become all too familiar with in the last five months. We're all just trying to navigate our battles, some more visible than others. Market America had valued employees and entrepreneurs in nine countries, so the world's problems were of keen interest to me—they were more like family members.

As I continued to read, briefly noting that all of these headline events had happened in thirty days, my thoughts drifted to the upcoming Leadership School event for Market America. I had to project strength and stability to thousands of entrepreneurs, ensuring them that the company was on solid ground despite the turbulent world around and within us. It was a daunting task. But one that I couldn't shy away from—not now, not ever.

I set down my laptop and took a deep breath, trying to gather my resolve. I was going to meet with Marc and the senior leadership team in an hour, and there were decisions to be made that only I could make now. But the first decision I had to make today was what the hell I would wear.

Facing the Challenges Head-On

Later that morning, Marc and I sat in the conference room, the weight of JR's absence hanging heavily in the air.

"Loren, we need to discuss the ongoing supply chain disruptions," Marc began, his tone serious. "Inflation is hitting us hard, and there are tensions in every one of the countries we're doing business with right now. It is causing all sorts of delays. It's affecting our UnFranchise Owners; sales are down. We're not the only company experiencing a downturn in sales. This economy is struggling right now. We need to come up with a strategy."

I nodded, trying to focus. The numbers didn't lie, but facing them felt like running through a lightning storm with an umbrella.

"I know, Marc. We also have to focus on promoting our business more than ever. Let's focus on the great things we offer to people. Digital transformation is better than worrying about ad processes here. Our e-commerce platform is struggling with the supply chain bottlenecks. Customers are frustrated. We have to stay focused on our UnFranchise Owners believing in the products we sell."

Marc leaned forward. "We've been investing in digital transformation, improving our online platforms, and integrating AI. But we need to do more to optimize operations. We have to introduce and promote new products."

"No! We have great products. JR and I built this company on great products. They work. We need our UnFranchise owners and customers to use the products and feel a change and then they can sell them. We don't need *new* products, Marc!" I yelled at him in a guttural tone, and I saw in his eyes that he was giving me a pass.

I sighed. "It's a lot, Marc. The hybrid work models, shifts in retail strategies, changes in consumer priorities…we must adapt to stay relevant. But I feel like I'm failing. I can't make decisions as quickly as I used to. I second-guess everything." Doubt had become an unwelcome companion I couldn't seem to shake.

Marc reached out and placed a hand on mine. "You're not failing, Loren. We're facing rapid regulatory changes and all kinds of consumer changes. It's a challenging environment, but we'll get through it. You don't have to do this alone." His words were soft, a reminder that I wasn't alone—even if it felt that way.

I looked at him, tears welling up. "I just want the team to step up, Marc. The whole team is not working to capacity. They need to step up."

Marc squeezed my hand. "We'll get there." His confidence was comforting, but I knew the road ahead would be anything but easy. How could I lead an organization of tens of thousands who were all individually mourning the loss of their thirty-year leader. How could I even begin?

Cracks in the Shell

As the days blurred into weeks, I stood in the kitchen, staring blankly at a carton of eggs. Cooking eggs had become my morning ritual, a small semblance of control in a world that felt so wildly out of it. But even that was a struggle. Scrambled or fried? Over-easy or hard-boiled? The decision seemed monumental, almost mocking in its simplicity. I was very aware I was milking it, extending this haggling over the style of my eggs for breakfast. But in the absence of JR, this morning ritual, as stupid as the decision seemed, gave me control and connection.

"Maybe I should just eat them raw," I muttered, half-joking, half-serious. It was a small rebellion against the overwhelming complexity of everything else in my life.

Each morning, cooking eggs became a metaphor for my internal conflict. The team at Market America was like the eggs—fragile, needing care, and needing to be broken to be transformed. JR had been the master chef, knowing exactly how to handle each egg and each team member. He had an innate ability to turn chaos into something extraordinary. Now, it was up to me, and I wasn't sure if I had the recipe right.

Testing the Recipe

I watched them closely in meetings. I could see the cracks in their confidence, the uncertainty in their eyes. They missed JR's steady hand, his unerring instincts. And a small, spiteful part of me reveled in their discomfort. If I had to struggle, maybe they should too—maybe that's how we'd all grow.

"Loren, we need to address the regulatory changes," one of the team members said during a meeting. "Data privacy and online business practices are becoming stricter. We must ensure compliance to maintain customer trust and avoid legal issues."

I nodded, trying to maintain my composure. Compliance was just one more ingredient to add to an already overflowing pot. "I understand. We also need to adjust our marketing strategies and product offerings to align with the shifts in consumer spending patterns. People are focusing more on value and necessity due to the economy."

"And our UnFranchise Owners—they are just not sticking to the ABCs. They are not sticking to the training." Another voice in the room served up.

They looked to me for guidance, but I felt like a fraud, a hollow shell trying to fill shoes that were too big and heavy. Imposter syndrome is real, and it doesn't care how long you've been at the top. I wanted them to understand my pain and see the gaping hole in my heart, but I also wanted my leadership team to rise above it, proving that JR's teachings had taken root. I wanted them to step up. And I knew that meant I had to step up—but I was so tired and hurt, and I felt too small.

Public Strength, Private Struggle

Despite the internal turmoil, I knew I had to show strength publicly. During Market America's Leadership School in early 2023, I stood on stage before thousands of entrepreneurs, my voice steady but my heart racing.

"JR was a legendary leader, not because he created an amazing business, but because he helped people do amazing things," I said, trying to channel his unwavering spirit. "Leadership School is our first major corporate event since JR's passing, and while the profound pain of his loss will always linger within us, so does his vision of a better future with prosperity for all."

I continued, "We've invested heavily in digital transformation, enhancing our online platforms and integrating advanced technologies. But more importantly, we are committed to our core values of sustainability and ethical consumerism. These values were at the heart of JR's vision and will continue to guide us forward." I spoke with conviction, hoping that if I said the words strongly enough, I'd start to believe them too.

On the outside, I tried to project the confidence that Rihanna had during the Super Bowl. I stood on stage, addressing thousands of UnFranchise Owners, ensuring the company was solid, that JR's vision for Market America was alive, and that JR's vision for Market America guided our every step. But behind the scenes, I was barely keeping it together—just trying to get through each day without breaking down.

One morning, as I stood in the kitchen, eggshells scattered across the counter, I realized that my grief was a part of the process. Like the eggs, I had to break open to let the raw, messy emotions spill out before I could begin cooking up something new. JR's impact was like the yolk—rich, essential, and binding everything together. Without it, I felt lost, but it was still there, nourishing me, even in its absence.

The Lesson: The Recipe of Grief and Resilience

Grief is like those eggs—fragile, messy, and demanding care. You can't avoid the cracks, the spills, or the chaos that follows. Just as an egg must be broken to reveal its potential, grief forces you to confront your rawest emotions before you can begin to heal. The process is neither neat nor predictable, but it is essential.

The rich and binding yolk symbolizes the love and impact that remains even after loss. It's the core of who we are, the part that nourishes us even when everything else feels shattered. In the kitchen of life, you may feel overwhelmed by the mess, doubting your ability to create something meaningful from the broken pieces. But it's in these moments of uncertainty and doubt that resilience is forged.

Resilience is about embracing the cracks, knowing they are part of the journey. It's about recognizing that the recipe of life doesn't always go as planned, but with patience, perseverance, and a little creativity, you can still create something beautiful. Even when the pieces are hard to put back together, you keep cooking and creating because that's where healing begins. It's not about avoiding the pain but transforming it into strength, one cracked egg at a time.

CHAPTER SEVEN

FIGHT, FLIGHT, OR FAINT

Time: Six Months AJRD

I SAT IN JR'S OFFICE, his leather seat worn and the cushion sagging from years of use during countless calls and meetings. His desk was still cluttered with notebooks and letters he'd written over the years. The weight of his absence pressed down on me, and my head throbbed with a dull ache that had become all too familiar in the last few weeks. My brain was tired from grasping at memories of JR, exhausted from fighting with family, friends, employees, and anyone else within earshot. It felt like I was constantly on edge, snapping at Amber, at the cleaning lady, at anyone who came too close to the whirlwind of emotions swirling inside me.

Worse still, I was frustrated with my team at Market America. The people we'd taught everything about the business seemed to be slipping, making decisions without me or around me. I knew they were trying to help, but I had two immediate reactions to each decision—*snap!*—and more questions. Why weren't they stepping up? Why were they making the easy decisions? Did they not think I could make the decisions? Was the business in more trouble than I thought? This constant barrage of doubts made me feel like I was losing control, not just of the company, but of myself.

Complacency had taken root in our company culture. At a time when we all needed to lean in and step up, some had either rested on their laurels or kept doing the minimum because they thought it was good enough. Perhaps they didn't realize that the absence of JR's larger-than-life presence meant that the standards were higher, not lower. I was keenly aware that Market America's ship needed a captain and a course to follow without hesitation. My insecurity in this fact kept me vigilant, so I snapped every time I caught the team slipping, every time an email went unanswered, and every time a task I asked for was still undone. The tension between the leadership team and myself was palpable, an unspoken rift that had formed since JR's death.

"I'll take care of it," Marc, the cool, calm leader who could find a solution for almost anything, tried to reassure me. He'd been handling nearly everything for me the last few months as I struggled not to drown in grief daily while learning the parts of the business that JR used to hold. But his words, meant to soothe, only deepened my frustration. Marc might as well have been trying to plug a volcano with a cork.

I sank my body into JR's chair, inhaling deeply, taking in the woodsy smell of leather, and looked around his office. This was the heart of our operation, the place where so many decisions had been made, and now it felt like a relic of the past, a museum exhibit rather than a functional workspace. His desk was the way forward, where the course could be plotted. But could I really do this alone?

My mind became clear and focused on the business—our entire company. Thirty years of business, eight hundred Market America employees, thousands of products, shipping worldwide. We started with a dream of a small office in a garage, and now we had offices in nine countries.

One hundred sixty thousand distributors, or UnFranchise Owners (UFOs), pay a small startup fee and earn money by selling our products instead of the traditional franchise setup where people pay into a corporation or brand to have a franchise. These UFOs market and sell our portfolio of exclusive products, including nutritional supplements, cosmetics, personal care, skin care, jewelry, and services directly to consumers. Our company provides all of the resources, technologies, and support to UnFranchise Owners to ensure their success. Market America wasn't just a company but an empire built on a dream. And I was the last person standing between it and potential chaos.

Suddenly, I felt goosebumps on my skin, like a cool breeze had wafted across the room. I could lead the fleet alone. But could I really? The question loomed large, a challenge that felt both terrifying and exhilarating.

I thought back to our past company events, where JR had brought his vision to life with passion and energy. Our Market America conferences were where we created and personified the true entrepreneurial spirit that powered our company. These weren't just events; they were the lifeblood of our business, where our dreams were shared and our future was forged. JR gave his whole self to everything he did—work, life, family, the dishes, telling the kids stories from Eagle Scouts every night, you name it. He didn't do anything halfway—he was loud about how he felt and what he wanted you to feel from him. Converting that level of all-encompassing belief in our company and in our current and potential Market America partners required more than canned speeches and PowerPoint presentations. JR created an experience.

Our conferences gathered our entire company, distributors, entrepreneurs, and employees into one place where we could convey our grand vision of how our company could change the global economy and create our own economy. Those were JR's famous words. We released new products, demonstrated new technology and systems, and trained our UnFranchise Owners on the principles and fundamentals to sell our products and to successfully build their businesses. Our biannual conferences were a three-day, ten-hour-a-day, intricately scheduled run of a show that included everything from executive speakers, successful UnFranchise Owners, guest speakers, and performances. And the occasional tightrope walk across Niagara Falls, running in a human hamster wheel, performing mental brain surgery, or a spaceship launch into outer space. These were more than just presentations; they were spectacles carefully orchestrated to ignite the entrepreneurial spirit in every person who attended. This conference became the wind beneath our UFOs' sails for the entire year forward. And ours also. We needed the events to recharge our own batteries.

JR threw his whole body across the stage at past conventions, sweating and giving orations like an Oscar-winning actor in front of thousands of people. He didn't just speak; he performed, making every presentation a dramatic, unforgettable experience. He ran across the stage, jumped down, hopped back on, skipped, kicked, and moved so fast that our producers had to put two microphones on him because one would inevitably fall off during his acrobatic presentations. He did whatever he could to encourage and irritate people to do something better with their life. He believed in irritation over motivation—believing people only changed when pushed to the edge of their comfort zone.

He created a life-size hamster wheel and would run in it frenetically to encourage people to get off the typical forty-five-year plan of working for someone else and retiring with a set income. He carried a sledgehammer and a clock to smash, expressing that we shouldn't be beholden to a schedule telling us when to go to work and when to leave.

"This clock is controlling your life," he'd say. "It limits you. It controls you. Let's take back our time!"

One of my biggest regrets is that when he asked me to do the alarm clock presentation at the thirtieth-anniversary conference, I told him I didn't have time. This regret lives inside me, fed by questions like…maybe it was a sign…maybe he asked me for a reason…maybe he needed to see if I could do the clock presentation, or if I understood its true meaning. I regret not making the time to honor his request then. I've smashed the clock on stage every time since.

As our conferences grew, so did the complexity of his presentations. JR dressed in a spacesuit and rocketed around space to demonstrate how people can dismiss an idea that might be seen as crazy or out of this world at the time—like putting a man on the moon or launching an online shopping company when the internet was in its infancy—until it's done, and then it becomes commonplace.

One of his most memorable presentations was when he hired performers from Cirque du Soleil to teach him how to walk a tightrope so he could walk across one on stage at one of our conferences—while pushing a wheelbarrow full of bricks. JR wanted to simulate the famous Charles Blondin tightrope walk across Niagara Falls in 1859, where the daredevil pushed a wheelbarrow full of bricks on live television. At the time, we all thought JR was absolutely crazy, but he was determined to prove a point.

JR set up his training area in a garage near our guest house in Miami, where I hardly ever visited, and practiced for two weeks with the trainer. He did this so I wouldn't find out and try to talk him out of it. No one knew he had planned this until he took the stage, and by then, it was too late to stop him. He climbed into a harness and stood on an elevated rope with the wheelbarrow handles in his hand in front of me, Amber, his three grandchildren, our closest friends, and thousands of our distributors. You could hear a pin drop.

He inched step by step, with determination etched on his face. I don't remember breathing as I stared up at him. The grandkids looked up at Pop Pop, praying he didn't fall. Amber wrung her hands tightly, shaking her head in disbelief. The crowd roared when JR reached halfway, in complete awe of his feat. But the noise was a distraction—he'd forgotten to wear earplugs, which the trainers told him were necessary to block out noise so he could keep his balance. A few more paces on the rope, and JR lost his footing. Bricks fell. The entire room gasped, but JR somehow regrouped and pulled himself and the wheelbarrow back on the rope. His hands shook as he pushed that wheelbarrow, but he kept moving, determined to reach the other side, even if it killed him.

All the theatrics, the drama, the nerve-wracking stunts weren't just to incite thrills—he wanted to drive home the point that you've got to believe the impossible can be done, even when the odds are against you. Even if you fall, even if failure seems imminent. You've got to believe you can do it. You have to think you can make it through and succeed.

"You just saw me do it!" He would say. "Do you believe I can do it again?" And of course, everyone would say yes. He would shout back, "Okay, who wants to be the first to get in the wheelbarrow with me?"

JR and I were magic on stage together, a perfect balance of passion and precision. We would work separately for weeks before conferences but meet before each one to swap notes. "Let me see what you're gonna say," he'd eagerly ask, so we were on the same page, and so he could tee up some of what I planned to say into his remarks. That collaboration, husband and wife, best friends, and mentors made me feel like we had the ultimate partnership.

When he watched me, it was like he was studying me, like a student watching a professor in a lecture hall. He would listen intently to my words and delivery. He'd clap at something I said, turning around to ensure everybody else was clapping too. I miss those moments. He'd mouth his reactions to certain things I said with approval. "That's a good one," he'd say, pointing, or "Yes!" with two thumbs up. When he was there, no matter what, I had a number one fan and cheerleader in the front row.

But then, just like that, my mind let the fog roll in. The clarity around leading the business was trapped in the fog without warning. My thoughts bobbled around like feathers at sea; some stuck to the surface, heavy and wet, while others picked up wind and floated gingerly just above the water's surface. Damn it. Why couldn't my mind stay focused on Loren Ridinger, the CEO?

The Roots of a Leader

I got my first job as an assistant at Sears by accidentally walking into the wrong office during a group interview session. My father demanded I get a summer job to keep me busy once school was out, and I spotted an ad in the classifieds for part-time jobs in the catalog department at Sears. It was supposed to be a simple summer gig, nothing more. I shuffled to their offices in downtown Greensboro, only to find two hundred other people also applying for the same job, which paid twice the minimum wage. The odds were against me from the start, and I wasn't even sure I wanted the job in the first place.

Eventually, I had to use the restroom. I stepped out of line and wandered through the cavernous building, winding past cubicles, storage rooms, and shipping and receiving departments in search of a bathroom. Finally, I found an unmarked door in a tucked-away corner, which I mistakenly thought was an available ladies' room. I pushed myself through the doorway. Inside, there was no bathroom. Instead, a man was sitting behind a desk.

"Oh, you're here for the job?" the man asked. "Yes," I said.

"Take a seat," he said. I did as he asked and interviewed for a managerial assistant job. I had no idea what the job entailed and no prior experience in that role, but I answered all of the man's questions, shook his hand, and was offered the job, which paid an excellent $7 per hour. Minimum was like $4 an hour back then. It was crazy.

I did the job well, but it didn't require me to speak in front of large crowds, much less convince people to buy into a brand-new company with a never-seen-before business premise. I was a worker, not a leader. At least, that's what I thought back then.

JR was an experienced leader with a big vision for a new kind of e-commerce company. He would go from city to city, state to state, telling everyone we would shop online one day.

"The future is people worldwide buying clothes, shoes, and makeup through their computers," he'd say. People will be able to shop without having to go to a store. He called it "the mall without walls," a concept that seemed as far-fetched as science fiction to most people.

When we launched in 1992, the world was a different place. Back then, online shopping was considered radical. Getting stuff delivered to your house in a couple of hours? Unheard of. Instacart? Please. We launched before AOL Instant Messenger, Uber, and Amazon.

"Believe it, Loren," JR said. "You'll be able to buy lipstick without going to a department store."

We started the company in our garage with two desks. My brother Marc was just starting college and worked with us after classes.

People were skeptical about our grand plan. At times, very few people even took our meetings—some of these appointments had maybe five to ten people, sometimes fewer, in the beginning. But JR had a vision, and he believed in himself.

I often drove him to these meetings, sitting in the back and watching with wide-eyed curiosity as he presented the plan. But I had never thought about selling people on his big vision myself. I saw their faces; some were confused, others simply did not buy it, and they were hesitant to believe in his idea for a different type of retail business. I'd walk away from some of those meetings questioning what we were doing. But every time, JR would say, "Great meeting, Loren!"

"Really?" I'd respond, skeptical if we were at the same meeting, perceiving the same response. "I'm not so sure they were into it. Those people didn't seem so excited."

JR looked me in the eyes and spoke. "Loren, it doesn't matter what they think. It matters what you think. Do you believe it? Do you believe in me?"

Then, one day, he turned to me as I drove us to our next presentation in San Antonio and said something that shook me in my shoes. "Today, you're going to show the plan." He didn't need me to present our ideas, but he wanted me to, apparently seeing some glimmer of talent I didn't see in myself. "You're going to talk about who we are," he told me. "Loren, you're the greatest speaker I've ever seen."

I looked at my boyfriend, bewildered. It was impossible that I was the greatest speaker—I'd never spoken in public! How could he have that unyielding belief that I was a great speaker when I'd never spoken in front of a crowd, much less in front of him?

My hands shook as I drove us to that meeting, my nerves frayed to near panic. The air was thick and hazy on a hot summer day. Sweat clung to my skin, a mix of humidity and sheer terror at the thought of what I was about to do. But a few hours later, I stood before a handful of people, their faces puzzled but curious about what I had to say. "Hi, my name is Loren Ashley—"

And that's all that came out of my mouth.

Then everything went black. I collapsed to the ground like a house of cards and passed out cold.

A few minutes later, I woke up to see half a dozen people looking down at me. JR fanned cool air across my face with a copy of our Market America sales deck. "Can you believe?" he screeched. "You're the greatest speaker, and they set you up to fail? They turned the air conditioning off! It's a hundred degrees out here! It's hot as hell! Anyone would have fainted in this heat! Get up!"

When I finally gathered myself, I figured he would never ask me to speak again. How could he ever ask me to present after I fainted during the presentation? But instead of letting me off the hook, he doubled his belief in me. "You're going to do it again. Tomorrow." He told me I was the best even after completely flopping in the meeting.

I sat in that car behind the driver's seat, stunned. After my abysmal performance, JR did not doubt I could be significant in front of people. His confidence in me was unshaken, even when mine was in tatters. I could feel the energy in his body projecting onto me, willing me to believe in myself too.

I made it to Houston. I stood in front of another half dozen people and presented the idea. I didn't faint. I cracked a smile or two. And I saw JR grinning from ear to ear, listening intently in the front row. His belief in me fueled every word I spoke, even as my nerves threatened to undermine me. I made it to the end, relieved as JR and the rest of the audience nodded in approval.

I made it through the following presentation and the next without medical assistance. I did it again in another city without distress. And again. And again.

Slowly, presenting in front of people became more routine. I became more comfortable engaging with our audience of distributors. JR's excitement and watching people connect with my words energized me. My confidence grew as the company grew, and after many years, I eventually came into my own as a speaker.

It only occurred to me after Croatia that JR had given me the greatest gift so many years ago when I fainted on that first stage. He gave me the gift of his confidence in me, like a seed that would eventually grow. I realized that his belief in me was the foundation upon which I had built my own sense of self-worth and ability. How could I not have had this clarity when he was still here, and I could have thanked him for it?

The Burden of Leadership

More weeks went by when my mind would go from crystal clear and blue skies to suddenly overcast, from where leading the business was second nature to where getting out of bed was a struggle. During these weeks of mental fog, I started noticing details about Market America's leadership team—details I'd overlooked when JR was steering the ship.

We grew Market America into a billion-dollar business with JR's vision. But JR was a seventy-two-year-old business executive of a tech company in an industry traditionally led by younger people, some of whom have never worked for others. In the months leading up to his death, JR was frustrated with some of our team, even our high-level executives, who thought they knew better and would change things we had put in place years ago, often without consulting us. Despite success, some people always think they can do better. They didn't doubt JR's leadership; their sense of success inflated their egos. They over-estimated their importance, believing they could manage everything without seeking advice. How did I know this to be true? Like some other execs, I was guilty of letting my ego get ahead.

Within our company, some thought they had all the answers. They would make moves without JR's input or make decisions JR didn't necessarily agree with, and JR would find out after the fact—and often have to clean up the mess they created. When JR told me about his feelings, I initially glossed over them instead of sharing in his anger. I spent much time explaining, "They don't mean any harm," instead of listening to him, letting him vent, or engaging with him long enough to validate his feelings. I wouldn't let his words soak in, perhaps because I knew and always knew how essential JR was to Market America's success. But now, in the harsh light of his absence, I could see clearly what he had been trying to tell me all along.

I began to hear about critical decisions being made—or ignored—without high-level approval. Without my approval. Had JR been here, things like budget plans, legal agreements, or distribution strategies would have never gotten approved without his blessing. I asked for an explanation from anyone, and I'd barely get a response. Until I'd finally be so livid about the situation, I'd call whoever I could find and flat-out ask, "What the fuck is going on?"

"We couldn't find you, so we decided on our own and kept it moving," they'd say.

Marc tried to reassure me again. "It'll be fine," he said. But his words, once a source of comfort, now felt like a Band-Aid over a gaping wound.

I watched our financials decline for weeks. Every week past JR's death, the numbers grew worse. It was like watching a slow-motion car crash, knowing the impact was inevitable but feeling powerless to stop it. I was upset with myself because I didn't listen closely to JR's concerns, and instead of siding with him, I told him not to worry. Now, I was more than worried. I was pissed.

I clicked open our latest financial report in my email, the first time I'd opened it in days. There it was again, another week where volume had dipped. Marc would have to continue to crack down on expenses to preserve and buy us time. He was an expert in this regard. But I knew the time for my forward contribution was needed. I rolled my eyes and looked up at a photo of JR and me from one of our events, holding hands, arms high, standing in front of a dozen team members. "I told you nothing happens here without you," I said. "We don't go on without you."

Tears welled up in my eyes. My lip trembled. My stomach burned, anger churning up in my belly. For weeks after JR's death, I felt stuck in neutral, too overwhelmed by my grief to move forward. But I couldn't sit back from work much longer. Market America is what JR and I had built for thirty years. It's home. It's where I belong. It's part of my DNA. Don't they know how much blood, sweat, tears, and sacrifice JR and I made to get us to where we are? I thought to myself, "I'm not going to ignore thirty years of hard work!" For the first time, after months of not knowing how to go back to work and feeling too overwhelmed to go back to work, I felt a spark. As if I had shifted into first gear, I released the clutch and started rolling forward. I had to find a way to remind our company of who we were, of who JR and I were, and if JR wasn't here to do it, then I'd have to do it. Somehow.

A Voice from the Past

I ran my fingers over one of JR's notebooks, staring at his signature loopy handwriting with bold letters. Words in all caps were sprinkled throughout the text for emphasis. Exclamation points ended sentences when he wanted you to pay attention to what he was saying.

A warm air wafted through the room, a strange sense of calm washing over me. My jaw was unclenched. My hands loosened around the notebook. The brooding anger I'd been bound to for months released me in a sudden moment. I knew something was happening, but nothing was happening simultaneously. I was alone, sitting in JR's desk chair. And then I heard it. Him.

"Loren, it's time."

I closed my eyes, feeling the weight of those words sink in. That memory of what happened in San Antonio the first time in front of JR flashed again. The fear, the uncertainty, the overwhelming sense of failure. I remember thinking that first night he asked me to speak, "If I ever get off this floor, I'm gonna break up with JR for making me get in front of these people and embarrass myself."

I eventually got up and made it back to our car. I was plotting how quickly I could get away from JR, sitting in the driver's seat, mortified by my epic fail in front of my boyfriend, disappointing the person who believed in me most. But JR immediately started making plans for our next presentation. "You were great today. And you're going to be great in Houston tomorrow. Let's go."

I opened my eyes. I saw a photo of our top leadership team and my family on stage at our thirtieth-anniversary Market America conference, the last one we did before JR passed away. There was Marc, hugging JR like an old college buddy, celebrating our making it thirty years in business together as if they'd just won the Super Bowl. Andrew, our vice president, whom I've known since he was twenty, who spent his whole career with us and is as close as a brother could get, stood next to Amber and the grandkids. My younger brother Steve, who's been with the company since we launched at just fourteen years old, was also there, along with Christian, a vice president I met when he came with his sister La La Anthony to a meeting about a makeup line and ended up getting a job offer on the spot after a thirty-minute conversation. Christian stood behind me on stage, looking protectively at JR and me. And JR, with his arms thrust in the air, smiling proudly at all we'd achieved. We were on top of the world at that moment.

I still had that financial report pulled up in front of me. My stomach flip-flopped again, and my finger started tapping furiously on the desk. This had to stop—my anger and the company's financial freefall. I had to stop it.

I had sat on the sidelines, stewing in sadness, anger, and confusion long enough. I wasn't clear about how to move forward, but our numbers weren't going to get any better if I sat here wallowing. I had to prove we were still a strong company. Someone had to steer the ship to its next great adventure. Almost like an agreement, it came again.

"Loren, it's time."

Reclaiming the Stage

So, I got up.

I clicked open the file of videos saved on his computer. I started watching his presentations, one by one, going back decades. I studied JR's cadence, how he moved from side to side, his vocal inflections, his rhyming verse, and anything I could take with me as I prepared my remarks to our company. I spotted Amber on stage in a few of those videos, and my mind started to recall memories of those years when we were building the company and we'd take her on the road with us from conference to conference. We seemed to have all the time in the world then.

I spent weeks reviewing notes, willing myself to get back on stage and communicate with our team. The more I worked on my notes, the more my stomach knotted with nerves. I didn't know exactly what to say. What if I broke down on stage? What if I pulled a San Antonio and fainted again? I didn't know if I could even make it through the speech. I spoke to myself daily in the mirror, willing myself to find the strength to move forward—for JR. For me.

I rehearsed. I cried. I prayed. I didn't feel ready.

But I kept going, driven by the memory of JR's belief in me. I looked at my notes, reread his quotes, and heard his voice again.

"Today is the day you step into your destiny, Loren. I believe in you."

Thousands of people were waiting for me to reaffirm the future of our company. People's livelihoods were at stake here. I didn't want to return to that stage; I had to. I repeated to myself, "I must do this."

When I woke up on Saturday, March 4th, it was six months after JR's death. Insecurity surged through me. The day's weight pressed down on me, making breathing hard. I thought, "I'm unsure if I can do this today." There were thousands of Market America UnFranchise Owners at an arena waiting for me to speak at our annual Leadership School, one of our two largest conferences of the year. The Miami Convention Center was already bustling with our guests ready to network, shop, and take in the energy of Market America. I got dressed and ready, but the reflection in the mirror was a woman I barely recognized—strong on the outside but trembling within. Then, I heard that voice again.

"You can do this. It's time to get up."

JR was cheering me on, just like he did when he would sit in the front row of the audience. He was still my champion.

It dawned on me for the first time that I had other champions too. My core group of friends—Amber, Mary, Natalia (who was bravely battling breast cancer), my brothers Marc and Steve, Christian, Lorena, Fat Joe, Serena, Jennifer, Alicia, La La, and others—became my informal board of directors. Over time, I had to distance myself from many others; I no longer felt comfortable with a larger circle of friends because I valued my time so much more dearly now. This tight-knit group provided the support and guidance I needed, helping me navigate personal and professional challenges. They were here with me now.

My heart raced as I went to the arena, reviewing my talking points for the umpteenth time. My white pantsuit kept me upright even if my confidence didn't. I didn't know if I would faint like I did in San Antonio some thirty-six years ago. But I made a pact with myself—show up, tell the truth, and do my best. I owed it to JR, to our company, and to myself.

Our team raced backstage, setting up cameras, adjusting lighting, and testing mics. The lights scorched hotter than usual, and the noise pierced my ears more. My hand trembled as I handed Christian my bag.

"Loren, it's time," Christian said. He grabbed my hand and started to walk with me. My favorite open-toed heels felt tighter than before, and I walked beside Christian at a snail's pace. My mind scattered in a thousand directions, none leading to the words I needed to say. I pursed my lips tightly together.

"Loren, you don't have to do this if you're not ready," Christian said.

There it was. An escape hatch. An emergency exit. I could leave. But what then?

"No," I whispered. "I'm here. Let's go."

I took a deep breath as they announced my name to the crowd. Badly broken. Mentally adrift. But me, unapologetically me. I stepped out onto the Market America stage, feeling the weight of thousands of eyes on me.

My voice trembled in the beginning. I held a tissue in my hand with a viselike grip. The audience was a blur of faces, all waiting to see if I would crumble or rise. I caught the eyes of my grandchildren sitting next to Amber, staring at me with love and concern, wondering if I would break on stage. Their innocent, trusting eyes anchored me. I spotted my dear friend Serena Williams from the stage, who flashed me a thumbs-up from the front row. "You got this," she mouthed to me.

A large image of JR appeared on the big screen behind me, and the crowd roared. It was like the beginning of a rock concert, and the crowd shouted words of love and excitement to the larger-than-life image behind me.

It was also a moment for me to smile up to JR as I raised my arm high, pointed to the heavens, and whispered only so he and I could hear, "I told you, baby. People will always need you. You're the one who gave them the belief. They believe in you still."

I stood for long seconds in front of the Market America family, this powerful fleet we'd become, and I tried to look each of them in the eye and give them a sense that he was still here with us. And that I was here with them too.

Then, I let the words come out.

"For the first time in my life, I am totally unprepared."

As I admitted that, a massive boulder came off my chest. It was true—I was unprepared to speak today and take over the company because I thought JR would live forever. But I continued.

My voice shook with every word. I soaked through a handful of tissues in between stories. I kicked off my shoes about halfway through the presentation, and the longer I spoke, the faster I paced the stage with each step. I spoke for two hours in front of my family, my friends, my grandchildren, our executive team, and all of our UnFranchise Owners. I caught looks of reassurance from some of them and concern for others. Amazement from a few. My delivery wasn't perfect, but my message was delivered: I was here. I was present. And this company was still strong.

"I want you to understand something. My heart may be broken. But we are not broken. This company is not broken. A broken heart can't break a company."

It felt like I was finally steering the ship back on course after months of drifting aimlessly through a storm.

I felt the energy in that arena shift from eager curiosity about my status, the company's status, and what the future of Market America was to confirmation, excitement, and hope. Looking into the audience, I saw what can only be referred to as a sea of love. I saw it on our UnFranchise Owners' faces, cheering in the crowd excitedly. In the first few rows, my team, sitting with my family, clapped and nodded in approval, moved by my heartfelt remarks and acknowledging that I was now fully present in running our company. They knew I was ready to emerge from the darkness. I had stepped back into the light—as a leader.

The Lesson: Embracing the Mantle of Leadership

Stepping into leadership, especially after a significant loss, is like navigating through a storm—you are tossed, turned, and often feel lost at sea. But true leadership isn't about having all the answers from the start. It's about finding the courage to stand up, even when unprepared, and trusting in the foundation laid before you.

In those moments of doubt, remember that the strength to lead isn't just about being confident—it's about being willing to carry on the vision passed to you. The belief others have in you can be the spark that ignites your confidence. And when you honor that belief, you create a legacy that is not just about survival but about thriving and guiding others to do the same.

Leadership isn't about perfection; it's about persistence. It's about showing up, even when you're scared, and finding the strength to steer the ship through the storm. Because in the end, the journey isn't just about where you end up—it's about who you become along the way.

CHAPTER EIGHT

TALKING, TAXES, AND TADPOLES

Time: Ten Months AJRD

The Call and the Chaos

THE PHONE RANG AT 7 a.m., its sharp insistence slicing through the early morning stillness. Fumbling to answer, still half-asleep, I thought about how overrated talking was.

"Hello, is this the person in charge of your household health insurance? I'd like to ask you a few questions about your insurance," a male voice echoed through the line, clearly reading from a script.

The skin on the back of my hand was dry and rough, scratching my eyelids as I rubbed them. The red standby light on the television glowed softly in the dim room. Where was this guy from? My throat felt as dry and rough as my hand.

"Hello? Are you in charge of your household health insurance?" the voice persisted.

The man took my silence as permission to read the rest of his script, rattling off statistics about the average cost of healthcare, our state's mortality rates, long-term care costs, monthly savings, government incentives—blah blah blah blah. The red light on the television held my gaze. When was the last time I even saw a bill for our health insurance?

"Ma'am, do you know how much you pay for health insurance every month? Or should I call back when your husband has time to share his thoughts?"

"I am." The words pushed out of my throat, scratchy and raw.

"Ma'am?" he said.

"I am."

"You are what, ma'am?" he repeated, clearly thrown off his script.

"I am in charge of our household health insurance decisions." The statement forced its way out, feeling like a thousand little cuts. "And we're doing just fine."

I hung up on him, rudely and abruptly. I didn't care.

Under the Water

The water ran down my body carelessly in the shower as my mind wandered. Bill payer. Accountant. Mimi. Pop Pop. CEO of Market America. Grieving widow. Lousy friend. Worse grandmother. The gardener, the captain, the plumber, the butcher, the baker—and even the fucking candlestick maker. There wasn't enough scrubbing to clean the muddied thoughts from my head. And no matter how often I swallowed water from the shower head, my throat remained dry and rough. I should suspend talking today. Of this, I was sure.

It had been almost ten months since Croatia—since it happened. I had already returned to the office as the sole leader of Market America, working with the team to ensure it kept growing. Every day was a race to the finish between learning new skills and managing my office. It was another jam-packed day with hardly any time to breathe. Every day, my bandwidth was at total capacity as I tried to handle my current responsibilities and take over JR's, a burden that felt heavier the more I learned about his side of the business.

"Can I get you coffee?" my assistant asked as I sat down and scanned my emails. There were 348 unread, which I tackled before my first meeting.

Before Croatia, I handled my areas of responsibility at the company—marketing and sales of our entire portfolio of products, holding trainings, and working with UnFranchise Owners—and assisted JR in whatever he needed. JR could need me to review a presentation, sit in on calls, or review product ideas for an upcoming launch on any given day. And when something wasn't working, JR would have me help problem-solve. If there were an issue with our sales team, he'd help me identify it, walk me through strategies to solve it, and help me execute it.

For the last few months, I realized that to keep Market America stable and growing, I would need to become an expert in all the areas JR used to handle. The catch-22 was that before if there was a problem at our company and he needed backup, I was the one person he leaned on to help solve it. Who was my backup?

"Loren, the bank's calling about the taxes. They're due tomorrow at 5 p.m."

Before Croatia, I knew very little about finances. I had never signed a personal check, only company ones. I never had to deal much with the bank or balance on our accounts. That was his job. JR manually paid every single check. Unlike your average billion-dollar tech company, which might have had the latest and greatest highly encrypted banking system, JR managed our personal finances by using Quicken. This old-school software has been around longer than Market America. He entered every expense, withdrawal, and payment manually. He never used online banking, not even for our finances. JR knew where every dime of our money went. How was I supposed to take over our company finances when I had never balanced a checkbook?

But I had to learn—and quickly. Despite the daunting task ahead, I was determined to equip myself with the necessary skills to manage our company's finances. I was ready to embark on a journey of learning and growth.

I sat with our accountants for days and got up to speed on our financial responsibilities and how to manage the payments. I leaned on Marc heavily to walk me through our accounting system. "Do we pay quarterly? Monthly?" I asked. "Which account do we pay these from?" I texted our accountants. Hell, I texted everyone to help me or at least help me hire the right people to manage the books. When I had to pay our personal income taxes, I had to ensure I knew the correct amount, how to write the check, and deliver that check to the right person.

"I'll get the check ready on my way to my last meeting," I texted my accountant, a sense of accomplishment and confidence in my ability to handle our personal financial responsibilities evident in my words.

I had six meetings on my calendar with our top UnFranchise Owners, who were rapidly growing their teams. Before Croatia,

JR used to have weekly calls and meetings with our distributors to dissect their business, identify shortfalls and opportunities, and give them strategies to implement. He was in tune with each one on a personal level. I marveled at how he could keep such minute information about hundreds of our distributors at his fingertips while managing the broader company.

"Hi, Dritan!" I chirped, his UnFranchise spreadsheets spread on my desk. Christian and Andrew sat across from me, taking careful notes. We all shared ideas and helped him map out a three-month plan to grow his sales of health and nutrition products to his network. He thanked us with smiles and air kisses as we hung up. "Who's next?" I asked. Another call was scheduled in three minutes.

The cadence of calls, emails, meetings, and questions came at me quickly. My plate was more than full; it was overflowing with the facts, data, processes, and information I had to digest. I walked through the halls dressed up in heels and accessories so everyone could see I was there to work. But as I passed a mirror, the reflection staring back was still that body with indentations in it, much more tired and now dragging a suitcase of emotional baggage so full it threatened to burst open at any moment.

My reflection taunted me in the mirror, confirming what I already knew—I was carrying too much. The weight of new responsibilities, grief, and memories had transformed into a massive, invisible suitcase strapped to my back. Each step grew heavier, the straps digging into my shoulders, making every decision feel like a Herculean task. The suitcase swayed with a life of its own, filled with restless shadows of the past, whispering doubts and fears. Yet only I could see it. To everyone else, I appeared poised, unburdened. I closed my eyes, feeling the spectral weight pressing down on me, and whispered to myself: stay focused. The only way to keep moving forward was to home in on what I needed to run this company, even as the suitcase threatened to crush me under its weight.

Financial Fears and Family Frustrations

"Did you like the color of the lipstick packaging?" Amber texted me. I'd just gotten off the phone with one of our vendors, confirming why a shipment wasn't delivered on time.

"Yes, honey. The one with the gold trim. Pops more on shelves." I was Amber's leader and her mother—I dropped everything to take a minute to answer her from my mind and heart.

Before I left the office, I grabbed what I needed to settle the tax payment. I looked at the payment amount again. "Is that right?" I thought. And how would I know?

I walked around the corner to JR's office and went into JR's computer to quickly scan JR's Quicken system. He had organized our personal finances by month and year. I scanned for the last tax payment he made before he died and cross-checked the numbers with the check he wrote out the last round of taxes. I made the necessary calls and decided the number was fair. I confirmed my meeting with the accounting team for tomorrow. What was our bank manager's name again? I felt another headache coming on.

The Aftermath of Unfinished Deals

Outside the office, I was also learning how to manage our personal finances, which were far more complex than answering questions from some surveys about health insurance. Before Croatia, JR was leading the sale of our New York apartment, and a buyer was lined up a few days from closing.

About a month after Croatia, the phone rang. "Mrs. Ridinger, we heard about what happened. Very sorry for your loss. I want to respect your time, so I'll just say that we have rethought our offer. Given your new situation in this economy, we feel that to close quickly, we'd need a price reduction of at least 20 percent. With your agreement, we could close in a few days, and I'm sure you'd want one less headache right now. Does this work for you?" The buyer was a polite ass.

Loren, preserve your words I said only to myself. Talk less. "Fine, let's get it to close. Goodbye."

I was short, direct, and impolite. I didn't care. Two months later the sale hadn't closed, and the buyer came to me a third time with a price reduction, which I approved, and the sale never closed because, ultimately, I discovered the buyer was trying to take advantage of the newly widowed me.

Another call flashed on my iPhone. This one was about our boat, *Utopia IV*, that I listed for sale after Croatia.

"Mrs. Ridinger, we want the boat. It's perfect for us. But honestly, we're stretching our budget more than it feels doable. Would you consider a small price reduction? We understand if that doesn't work for you." His voice was even, almost shy, and earnest.

I cleared my throat. Still rough. Still dry. Use fewer words, Loren. "No."

This sale never went through either.

As I dragged myself to breakfast, simultaneously checking emails, a note from my accountant came in with the subject line: "Quarterly Performance Review of Ridinger Portfolio." I was always cc'd on these emails, but JR handled the reviews. In the months after Croatia, I spent more time talking to my accountant than my closest friends. I was learning to be JR in all our financial dealings. It was like returning to school for a girl who never wanted to think about money.

On a call later that morning, my accountant emphatically said, "Loren, you must be on top of your accounting department at Market America. Otherwise, people may try to get over on you. And even if they don't, small mistakes overlooked turn into massive cash losses. We'll talk about it next week at our weekly meeting."

Hanging up the phone, I leaned into the hallway mirror to adjust my earring, which was hanging on for dear life. There she was again—the woman who looked just like me but with a body that seemed to hollow out a little more each day. The suitcase was there, bulging with unseen weights, its presence a constant reminder of the burdens I carried. It hovered just behind my reflection, its locks clicking open and shut, as if mocking my attempts to keep it closed.

My mind drifted again, and the suitcase began to swell, spilling out spectral forms of tax documents, bank statements, and accounting spreadsheets that fluttered around me like ghosts. Their whispers filled the air: "Did you send flowers to La La for her birthday? Did you call the bank about the beneficiary statement? Did you even shower this morning? And what is that spot on your left cheek?"

Focus, Loren, focus.

I tried to concentrate, but the forms circled faster, becoming a whirlwind of demands and doubts. Each ghostly paper tugged at my thoughts, making it harder to think clearly. Anger started to rise, hot and fierce, as I reached out to grab the swirling forms, but they slipped through my fingers like mist.

I left the mirror and headed into the office. We were in the middle of planning several large initiatives. Marc, Andrew, and Christian would just come here and find me if I was five minutes late.

I was exhausted from learning the ins and outs of the business and our finances, but I felt stronger with the new knowledge that allowed me to lead more confidently. I sat taller in my office chair, my eyes dry from scanning documents and bloodshot from crying between calls. I was leading with more confidence than in previous months. Or at least attending meetings without hanging up on people or cursing at my staff or myself when I became frustrated at how much I had to take on.

Clarity and Control

During this time, I became addicted to clarity. Clarity forced me to have honest conversations with myself. I was angry about losing JR, but I had to ask myself why I was yelling at everyone at Market America. As the organization's leader, was I unclear about what I needed? What did the company need? Did I simply need additional help? What more did I need to learn? What was I missing? How fast could I learn it?

The bulging suitcase in the mirror's reflection wasn't just my emotional baggage or filled with my uncontrollable tears—it was a living, breathing entity. Since Croatia, my capacity had shrunk, and the suitcase had grown in proportion, its seams straining and threatening to burst. It didn't just hold my burdens; it also held the remnants of JR's life, his unfinished tasks, and his lingering presence.

I saw the reflection in the mirror—a woman with hollowed eyes and a weary smile, standing beside a suitcase so full it seemed ready to explode. It pulsated with a life of its own, whispering the weight of unspoken words, untaken breaths, and undone deeds. I could almost see the memories and responsibilities writhing inside, pressing against the fabric, desperate to escape and overwhelm me.

Living both my life and the life JR left behind felt like trying to walk with one foot in the present and one in the past. The suitcase was moments away from spewing its contents, spilling secrets and sorrows for the world to pick through. My reflection seemed to plead with me, urging me to make space to lighten the load.

With a reduced capacity, clarity became my savior. It was a sharp blade cutting through the chaos, revealing what mattered. I started by clearing my agenda of unnecessary noise, politely declining meetings I didn't need to attend. I consolidated or eliminated anything that took up extra space in my life. Running the company, leading my family, and dealing with devastating loneliness, I'd run out of room for nonsense.

In the mirror's depths, I saw not just a tired woman but a resilient one. Loren, the leader. Loren, the mother. Loren, the widow, who carried on despite the weight of two lives pressing down on her. My reflection, framed by the bulging suitcase, reminded me that even when burdened, I could find clarity, purpose, and strength to move forward.

The Road Ahead

Arriving at the office a short time later, I joined the Zoom call where dozens of leaders were waiting for me to start the meeting.

"Hey, guys. Where are we at today?" I sat at my desk in my office, ready for the day's business. Right after JR died, these Market America calls were triggering, and I was talking with people who couldn't understand my grief or the distortion it was causing inside me. People who demanded answers I didn't have at the moment. Quickly, phrases like "I can't," "I don't know," "I don't fucking know," or "Can't you figure this out yourselves?" flew out of my throat like angry birds. The calls were rough on everyone. I'll be the first to say it: I was a disaster. But thanks to clarity—I now knew who I needed to evolve into. Before talking on this call, I interviewed myself quickly.

"Loren, what's happening here? Why can't we just forget the grief for a second? Let's tackle the real problem. The real problem is your team's not performing. What do we do about it? How do we change it?"

My words softened for the first time since Croatia. I greeted people with a nicer, softer approach.

"It looks like sales for our next event are a bit soft," the voice on the other line said.

"Okay. What do we need to solve it? The entire team is not performing at the level we need. So, how can we rally and solve for this?"

At an all-hands-on-deck company meeting, leaders started chirping like birds—lots of talking but no clear thoughts. I leaned forward into the Zoom camera, breathed in, and began. "I don't want to be upset anymore about our team. I've been upset. I've been angry for the last ten months. I'm sad. I can't fix anything I've said in the past. But let me just tell you something. I love you guys. We've been together for thirty years, but I need you to step up."

My voice was clear, and my eyes focused forward. I had another call in five minutes that I had to prepare for. I had no time for excuses, chitchat, or "But wait!" I had made a decision, and I had to stick to it. I outlined the changes I'd be making to how the team reported to each other and the level of accountability I would implement as the new gold standard.

"No, you don't have to do that!" a senior leader said, interrupting. "Why, Loren?"

"Because I'm doing things I never expected to do. I'm learning and doing what JR handled in addition to my previous roles. You all need to evolve with me so our company thrives," I explained.

"But this? I've been with you forever! I've been with JR forever! I don't need to be managed differently!"

"Again, I love you," I said, my voice steady. "But I'm in the fight of my life right now. And if you can't show up for me or JR when we need you to move, then I need to rethink the players."

Drawing boundaries with people who had worked for us for decades, become family, and were desperate for assurances I couldn't promise was agonizing. But clarity kept me focused on the bigger picture; my capacity would not increase, so changes had to happen for us to survive. Before JR's death, I would give them the benefit of the doubt, time to make good and do better. Now, I didn't have the space to allow for underperformance. I had to take a harder position with people than ever before. Some didn't like that; some weren't used to it. Boundaries forced me to stay focused on the bigger goals, the higher priority. I put the most essential things in my limited bandwidth. For the company, the priority was getting our numbers back on track.

From speaking at our Leadership School in March and working daily with our team, I slowly started feeling more grounded in the work. Each conversation I could have without a breakdown felt like a triumph. I spent more time with our team, employees, and distributors, and the more people I connected with, even just for five minutes to pick up a document, the more at ease I felt. Our company felt recharged after Leadership School, energized by being together in Miami, seeing each other, making new friends, laughing, and connecting with people. It was what JR enjoyed most about our company, and in between our larger conferences, if there was one thing that always helped us build our business, it was meeting with people face to face. Meeting new and existing UFOs, listening to their needs, coaching them, guiding them, and equipping them with the tools to empower their own growth was arguably the most enjoyable part of our journey.

After months of calls and meetings and diving deeper into every aspect of Market America, I decided it was time to hit the road. In early January of 2024, we scheduled a multicity tour of over twenty cities to meet our people in the field, attract new people to our business, conduct live brainstorming and mentoring, reconnect with our distributors in the field, and let them know that the company they've been a part of is still thriving.

During the first few dates, I was vulnerable and transparent. Perhaps a twinge of anger still overpowered my voice as I spoke, but I pushed myself to be as passionate as possible to reignite that belief in our distributors. As the tour progressed, talking became easier, not enjoyable, but easier. I spoke with more kindness and clarity, still preserving my words. I let them see my vulnerability and my raw side. My day-to-day function seemed more rhythmic, and the more I worked, the more I could bury myself in it, distracting me from the grief, even if for a few hours. Being with the UnFranchise Owners community was what made me the happiest, as it had when JR was alive, reassuring and uplifting to them. It was when I was at the office that I would snap. Being on tour brought out the best of me and I started to snap less at the office. I was happy to be with the UFOs again and out in the field where JR and I had always lived with them…traveling and growing with our leaders.

In my personal life, the most important thing was family. Being a better mother to Amber and a better Mimi to the grandkids meant prioritizing my time and spending it the way I wanted, without outside distractions.

Tadpoles and Transitions

The phone finally stopped buzzing around 6 p.m. I had been answering questions all day. "What should we do about this?" "How much of that do you need?" "Can we do this?" Decisions, decisions. My temples throbbed.

I walked back into my house, the silence almost deafening after the day's chaos. I dropped my bag and felt the day's weight slip from my shoulders. As I moved through the house, everything was still exactly as I had left it that morning, a stark contrast to the whirlwind of my thoughts. My mind drifted back to that intrusive call from the morning. Should I reconfirm that my number is still on those Do Not Call lists? The question lingered, adding to the day's frustrations.

Suddenly, another notification chirped from my phone, breaking my thoughts. It was a FaceTime call from Amber. I quickly answered, trying to steady my emotions. "Hey, honey," I said, forcing a smile.

"Hi, Mom," she replied warmly. "Ayden has a question for you."

I watched as she passed the phone to my grandson. Ayden's face lit up the screen, his eyes wide with excitement. He was wearing plastic gloves and holding a beaker. "Mimi, when will you see the tadpoles Pop Pop and I grew in the aquarium?"

A wave of bittersweet emotion washed over me. JR had adored playing with his grandkids. He loved getting down on the ground with them, getting dirty, and doing science experiments. He was constantly uncovering species of animal life in the backyard. He'd had a huge science lab installed in our house so the kids could conduct experiments as if they were rocket scientists, stocked with dozens of fish so that he could teach the kids all about ocean life.

I remembered the day he and Ayden brought home a hundred frog eggs. JR was like a kid himself, full of excitement and hope. They were going to watch them hatch and grow into something marvelous. The details were a mystery to me—I had never bought tadpoles. But JR's enthusiasm was infectious. He had a way of making every moment an adventure.

"I'll be there soon, Ayden," I said, my voice catching slightly. "We'll check on those tadpoles together."

Ayden beamed, his joy evident even through the screen. "Okay, Mimi! I can't wait!"

I put the phone down and took a deep breath. JR's legacy lived on in these small, everyday moments. His spirit was present in the aquarium, science experiments, and our grandchildren's laughter.

I walked over to the aquarium in our apartment and peered into the water. No tadpoles were swimming here, but gold and blue fish were swimming in circles. The sight brought a tear to my eye and a smile to my face.

At that moment, I realized among all my new titles, I had to leave space to be a marine biologist for Ayden.

The Lesson: Embracing the Chaos and Finding Purpose

Life after loss isn't just about finding balance but redefining it. The world doesn't stop spinning when your life is turned upside down—it speeds up. You're suddenly juggling responsibilities you never imagined would be yours, and the weight of grief makes everything feel heavier. But here's what I've learned: it's not about mastering the chaos but embracing it. The chaos is where you discover what truly matters, what you can let go of, and where your strength lies.

In my grief, I realized that leadership isn't just about guiding others; it's about leading yourself through the darkest times. It's about making tough decisions with a broken heart and still finding the courage to show up, even when you feel like you're failing. I had to learn to prioritize not just the needs of my company but also my own well-being, my family, and the legacy JR and I built together.

Clarity doesn't come from waiting for the storm to pass; it comes from standing in the eye of it, facing it head-on, and deciding what you will fight for. Whether it's ensuring the future of Market America or simply taking time to marvel at tadpoles with my grandson, it's about making intentional choices that align with my core values and what nourishes my soul.

So here's the truth: life will never be the same. The old balance is gone, and the new one is fragile and ever-changing. But within that fragility, there is power. The power to redefine your life, your purpose, and how you show up for those you love. It's not about perfection; it's about progress. Every step forward, no matter how small, is a victory. And every moment of clarity, no matter how fleeting, is a gift.

So embrace the chaos. Let it teach you, shape you, and reveal the strength you didn't know you had. Because in the end, it's not about how well you juggle—it's about what you choose to hold on to and what you're brave enough to let go of.

CHAPTER NINE
BULLSHIT ADVICE

Time: Fourteen Months AJRD

PEOPLE OFTEN OFFER CLICHÉD ADVICE when someone dies. Phrases like "time heals all" are thrown around, but let's be honest, they're just empty words. Time doesn't heal anything. It's just a relentless force pushing us forward, indifferent to the pain it leaves in its wake.

When you lose someone or something you love, you realize a simple truth: You will continue to exist, with time acting as the relentless current that keeps you moving through still and rough waters. Time has terrible bedside manners; its hands are cold and impersonal as they push you forward, never pausing for your sorrow.

Several months had passed since JR died, and time had brought me nothing but an ever-changing ocean of emotions. I was adrift, unable to find solid ground, constantly fighting against the current. On a particularly humid, sticky Wednesday afternoon in Miami, I found myself pissed off at times, more than I had ever been. The air was thick and oppressive, clinging to my skin as I forced myself to walk into a nondescript downtown office building that I'd driven by a million times but never had a reason to go inside. The grief counseling group session Serena suggested I go to was in Multipurpose Conference Room B on the third floor of this high-rise.

Grief in a Conference Room

The setting couldn't have been more unexpected. Was I there for therapy or to do my taxes? The sterile, scentless air of the room only added to my discomfort. I hesitated, wondering if it was the right time to share my story with strangers. I wasn't ready to give them access to my tears. I almost turned and walked out before I even sat down.

Serena's voice echoed, "You've tried everything else, Loren. Just go to one group session."

She was right. What's one more group session in the line of tactics I could try? I had hired and fired five therapists, the last one because she suggested I start dating again. Dating? Was she out of her mind?

In Room B sat a group of visibly unhappy women in a semicircle—some surprisingly young enough to be my daughter, some old enough to be grandparents like me. The contrast between them was jarring. Several looked like they'd just left Prime 112, with designer bags, shoes, fresh highlights, and blowouts. A few looked like they were wearing grief like a heavy cape, an ever-present shadow.

Sitting beside a woman in a red blouse holding her purse close to her chest, I took a deep breath. Why did the air have no scent? It smelled sterile. Is this what losing everything smells like?

A phrase from Joan Didion's *The Year of Magical Thinking* flashed like a neon sign in my mind. "People who have recently lost someone have a certain look, recognizable maybe only to those who have seen that look on their faces." It was true. In the curves of their faces, the tiny hairs shooting in every direction from missed eyebrow appointments, and in the softened skin below their eyes weathered by tears, I could see the feeling of unbearable loss, just as I was feeling it.

The Collective Grief

Our group facilitator, a tall man in a sports jacket, entered the room and sat at the semicircle's head. "Share your names and how you're feeling today," he instructed. His voice was gentle, but I was anything but at ease. I pursed my lips together, trying to drown out Serena's voice. Time brought me to Room B, knowing I wasn't ready to share a word. Crossing my arms, bracing for these strangers' inevitable tears and sob stories, I took one more deep breath, still smelling nothing.

As they shared their stories, it became clear that we all had one thing in common—we were still profoundly hurting, maybe permanently. Time had done little to heal any of us. Some of us in Room B had arrived just after a few weeks, and some after a few years of losing everything. It didn't matter how much time had passed; the pain was still raw. The woman in the red blouse spoke first. "He did everything; he cared for me," she said. The lady wearing a Nike tracksuit sitting almost opposite me spoke up. Her husband died of a heart attack in his sleep.

"I have to get a second job," she whimpered, "or else my kid will have to come out of school."

My Guard Crumbles

As these women shared their stories, my guard began to crumble. We'd all lost everything. For some of us, it was more than one "everything." We'd all lost significant and irreplaceable people in our lives. For me, it was my lover, my husband, the father of my child, and Pop Pop to my grandchildren, my coach, my confidante, my best friend—my everything.

But these women also lost their providers, safety nets, and solid ground. One lady spoke about a business partner leaving suddenly after two decades and how the betrayal felt just as crushing even though they weren't family. "He was my work husband, and I spent more time with him than with my children." Her words struck me. She had lost her entire business, unable to recover after the split, financially or emotionally. Grief wrapped around us in ways you only understand when it happens to you. Like pieces of a puzzle, hearing these women bearing their raw truths started putting things together for me.

"Loren, would you be willing to share your story today?" Mr. Sports Coat singled me out, and all eyes in the semicircle landed on me.

I felt JR's presence, watching me, urging me to speak. I cleared my throat, swallowed my spit, and looked at each person in the semicircle. Fondling my wedding ring between my thumb and finger, I spoke.

"My story is that JR and I built our dream life. The company we founded, Market America, was thriving and steadily growing domestically and internationally. Our company took thirty years to build. It provided a life and a home, many homes for me, my family, and hundreds of UnFranchise Owners. We all could live out our dreams because of JR's dream so many years ago. We've made a lot of money together—a lot. And more importantly, we've been helping thousands of people worldwide take control of their financial destiny. Our family is healthy and happy. We traveled together. We did everything together—except for skiing. I hate high altitudes. He went skiing once a year without me, though he'd beg me to go with him. So for twenty-four hours a day, seven days a week, 365 days a year, we were together—except for those four days. I admit, I needed the four-day break—I wouldn't go out. I bummed around with greasy hair. It was great!"

What was I saying? Unplanned, unpolished, unlike me… the words of my story took on their own life.

"It was our time. Until it wasn't."

That part of my story came out of my mouth smooth and steady, like I was narrating someone else's life. Everyone in the room looked, wondering if they should stay quiet or say something to console me. I inhaled Room B again. And the tide came flooding to shore.

"And I'm so incredibly pissed off! Instead of living my dream life with my soulmate, after loving him so hard so nothing could ever separate us, I'm sitting here with you people. I'm drowning in loneliness. My sadness is so constant that I'm always struggling to breathe normally. And I'm exhausted from how much anger and guilt I'm carrying around. And this sucks. All of it." I took another breath. "This room. This whole room. It smells like pity. And I hate it. I hate it. Fuck!"

The room was silent.

In what felt like hours, we all just stared at each other. Waves of emotions rolled onto shore and pulled back out, dragging debris back and forth between us. I had no words left, no more of my story to tell Room B. I focused on how my wedding ring felt between my fingers as Mr. Sports Coat decided how to lead us off this rocky shore.

The Turning Point

Time brought me to Room B to face new emotions: humility and empathy.

With a new lens, I looked at these women and focused on the hurt and worry on their faces. I thought about my life since JR died almost a year ago. For the last several months, I had been hiding at home. I worked in a haze. I was trying to figure out what I was doing, what to do, or where to go. I couldn't handle thinking about the business most of the time. But I wasn't worried about money or how I would live securely. Whether or not I took advantage of them, I had plenty of options. I had a fantastic support system, and despite the expansive and ever-present loneliness I carried daily, I felt loved. And here I was, frozen, afraid.

I looked around and then up. I was sure JR was watching this scene play out.

Sitting next to women in need of a solid place to land, some way to take care of themselves in their future, I started to feel a spark inside me, like a little jump start. Seeing those women fearful about their survival gave me a reason to get out of my head and put grief on a temporary shelf, even for this short hour. In this semicircle, I rediscovered my "why."

One woman, Teresa, caught my attention. She clutched a designer bag, a gift from her late husband, which now seemed like a symbol of everything she had lost. Her eyes were puffy and red, yet she spoke with a soft determination. "We were married for eighteen years," she began, her voice trembling. "He was my rock, my provider. Now, I must learn to live without him, like every part of life, and it terrifies me."

Her words resonated deeply with me. I remembered how JR had been my rock, not just in our personal lives but also in our business. I had leaned on him for so much, and now, like Teresa, I had to learn many things.

Beside her sat Monica, a young mother of two. Her husband had died in a car accident just six months ago. "I don't know how to be both parents," she admitted, tears streaming down her cheeks. "I have to find a job, but I've been a stay-at-home mom for so long. The thought of leaving my kids to work breaks my heart. And I don't know how to be their dad; they need someone to do that for them. I'm not enough."

Monica's struggle mirrored my feelings of inadequacy. I had been so consumed by grief that I had neglected my responsibilities at Market America as a mother and as Mimi. The realization hit me hard—I needed to be there for others.

Then, there was Alice, an older woman who had lost her lifelong partner. She was in her seventies and had no immediate family. "We had plans for our next chapter," she said, her voice barely above a whisper. "Now, I'm facing those years alone. The house feels so empty without him. I'm too old to start over, so I feel like I'm just waiting, waiting to die next."

Alice's loneliness was palpable, reminding me of the isolation I had imposed on myself. I had withdrawn from my colleagues and friends, shutting out the support system crucial for my healing and the company's continuity. I didn't mean to do so, it just happened because I wasn't vigilant. I remember conversations with myself that focused on reuniting with JR on the other side. I would argue that if I could be 1000 percent sure I would find him waiting for me on the other side and we could continue our life together, I would have found a way to get to him. I never fully understood deep depression until I was more than drowning in it. You can't until it happens to you.

The Realization

Each story was a thread in the intricate tapestry of grief that connected us all. These women had lost not only dear people but also their sense of security and identity. They were navigating uncharted waters, just as I was.

I took a deep breath and interjected, much to everyone's surprise, "JR and I founded Market America to help tens of thousands of people build their success. People come to Market America to create something for themselves; they want financial independence no matter their reason for pursuing it. I have forgotten that lately. Market America is more than a lifeline for thousands of people; it is a map for people to follow and chart their dreams. It's why JR was so passionate and dedicated to the business. It is why I still am." The women nodded in understanding. They didn't need to know the specifics of my wealth or business. They needed to hear that someone else understood their pain and would help them.

In Room B, we were all connected by grief, but many of these women lived in fear of the unknown. What comes after you lose everything? And this, I knew instantly, was my "why" in this room and beyond.

As I continued making circles around my wedding ring with my forefinger, it became almost like a dial or a compass, and the semicircle became focused like a vast horizon. I could help the strangers in Room B find a lifeline too. Not by giving them a job per se, but by understanding what they were feeling when others who have not lost simply cannot. I could reenter the world by listening a little closer to people's stories and acknowledging that they are as devastating to them as mine. I could go out into the world and help people create opportunities for themselves so that no matter the loss, there was not this paralyzing fear.

I cleared my throat and spoke again, this time with more determination. "We all have our battles, and we all have our strengths. My daughter, Amber, told me something I will never forget. She said, 'I lost both of my parents, and I'm grieving. My father passed away and is no longer here, but I also lost my mother because although she is still here, she is not the same and never will be. I'm learning to live with and love this new version of my mom harder.'" My voice cracked, I dropped my head, and the woman beside me put her hand on my shoulder. Amber's sentiment resonated with everyone sincerely. Loving someone so intensely as I did means that when they're gone, a part of you is irrevocably changed. But it also means that you must reinvent yourself despite the loss for yourself and those around you who still need you. That, we collectively agreed, is the scariest part of being the survivor.

Serena's insistent and beautiful face popped into my head. She'd encouraged me to go to a group therapy session and be around other people, other women, who'd lost someone. "Maybe something will come out of it," she said. And so it did. Thank you, my friend.

It was time for me to shift back into high gear. I was ready.

I think time is a bitch, and I still hurt every day in every way a human heart can suffer. And I know that I don't know how long all these emotions will rule me; I'm prepared for it to be forever. But there was a spark again. JR is watching, and I will honor him—our forever leader.

A Letter to JR

I didn't spend much time with those ladies in Room B. Still, their stories will stay with me forever, fueling the tiny spark that inspires me to move forward.

I've found that to get through the most significant loss; you must let everything go and see a reason to make your time matter again. That reason, that "why," will save you and keep you from drowning.

Time snickered, "Finally!" Grief mumbled, "I'm still here." And JR's voice whispered, "I love you, Loren."

I went home that night and wrote JR a letter.

Dearest JR,

There's something I need to say that's been weighing on me. I never asked you what I was supposed to do if you were gone before me. Even though you were eighteen years older, I never thought it would be you before me. It never crossed my mind—not even for a moment. It's ironic, isn't it? We talked about it forever. But forever isn't what we got.

I remember thinking about asking you that question earlier in our relationship, maybe around the fifteen-year mark. But I didn't. I didn't want to put that energy out there to jinx us in some superstitious way. So I never asked, and you never brought it up. I remember once, I suggested getting a beautiful monument for our family so we could be buried side by side. You laughed and said, "I think we should talk about that. We'll live on, even though we're not in the same body. We'll scatter our ashes in beautiful places." That one time, so many years ago, was the only reason I knew you wanted to be cremated. I had to cling to that memory because I never asked you anything else about it.

I didn't ask where you wanted to be laid to rest, how to handle the bank accounts, or if there was anything hidden I should know about. I didn't even know about the $13,000 stuffed in the zipper of your briefcase from our trip to Croatia until I found it. You always felt insecure without having cash on hand because of how you grew up with nothing. And now, here I am, torturing myself over every decision, wishing we'd had that conversation about what I'm supposed to do now with our family, our money, your ashes, the business, and even your cologne.

About five years ago, I asked again about us being buried together, thinking we'd share a resting place. But you reminded me, as always, that you didn't want to be in graveyards and stones. You wanted to be free, to scatter our ashes. You said, "We're going to talk about this one day, but we're not going to worry about being buried." I wish I had been more persistent. Maybe you trusted me to make the right decisions, knowing I knew you well enough to honor your wishes.

But, JR, these conversations are meaningful for most people because grief isn't normalized. We don't talk about it in school; we don't discuss how to get through it. It's real life, and because of that, people avoid it. And then, they're left like me, questioning every move. Should I keep the house? Would you be mad if I sold it? What would you want me to do?

I wish we'd talked about it more. Maybe then, I wouldn't feel so lost now. But despite all this, I promise I'm doing my best to honor you and make decisions you will be proud of. And I hope, wherever you are, you know that.

I'll love you forever,
Loren.

Another letter I should have written when he was still living.

The Lesson: Rediscovering Your Purpose Amid Grief

Let me tell you something I've learned, something I had to discover the hard way. Grief, like time, doesn't wait for you to catch your breath. It doesn't pause for your tears or give you a moment to gather yourself. It's a storm that rages on, and if you're not careful, it can pull you under, leaving you gasping for air. But here's the thing: within that storm, there's an opportunity to rediscover who you are and why you're here.

When I lost JR, I felt like I lost everything. My anchor, my purpose, my reason for waking up each day. I know many of you have felt the same—whether through the loss of a loved one, a dream, or a part of yourself. It's easy to feel like the world has ended like nothing will ever be the same. And you're right—it won't be. But that doesn't mean your life has to stop. This is your moment to ask yourself the most crucial question: Why am I still here?

For me, the answer came when I least expected it, in a sterile conference room surrounded by women who had also lost their everything. It wasn't about the business, the money, or even the legacy JR and I had built together. It was about something more profound—a commitment to myself and others. I realized that despite the pain, I was responsible for finding a new purpose for those around me and myself. I want to turn my grief into something that could help others. To make my time matter.

So, what's in this for you? It's simple: You have the power to redefine your story, even in the wake of unimaginable loss. You have the strength to transform your grief into a new beginning, a new purpose that honors what you've lost while embracing what you still have. It's about taking that pain and using it as fuel to move forward, rebuild, and rediscover the "why" that will guide you through the storm.

Ask yourself, what is your "why"? What is that one thing that can pull you out of the darkness and give your life meaning again? It doesn't have to be big or world-changing—sometimes it's as simple as deciding to live fully for yourself and those who still need you. But make no mistake: finding your "why" is the key to surviving and thriving after loss. It will keep you grounded when everything else feels like it's slipping away.

You're not alone in this. I'm walking this path with you, learning, stumbling, and rising again. And I want you to know that if I can find my way back to purpose, so can you. Grief may have its hold on you, but your life, time, and purpose are yours to reclaim. Take it one day at a time, and remember: your best life is still ahead of you, even after losing your greatest love. It's your birthright to find that life, to live it fully, and to make every moment count.

This is your journey, your time, and your life. Claim it.

CHAPTER TEN

BETWEEN THE DASH

Time: Thirty Years BJRD

SOME MOMENTS IN LIFE DEFINE us, shaping who we are and what we become. They are the moments that carve out the spaces between the dates on a tombstone—the dash that tells the story of our lives. This dash represents the time we spend living, the experiences we accumulate, and the choices we make. Looking back now, I can see how big and small moments pushed me towards the life I was destined to live.

The Beginning of the Dash

The summer I turned sixteen and accidentally landed a great position at Sears, I learned that life had a way of surprising me. It was more than just a job; it was my first taste of success and ignited a fire in me that has never burned out.

High school was a different story. It was a time when I felt invisible, overshadowed by the wealthier kids whose parents could afford the latest fashions and trends. My family didn't have money for the designer jeans that would have made me feel like I belonged. I wore imitation Jordaches from Sears, constantly feeling less than the country club girls. My mother tried to build me up, but inside, I struggled with my identity and our circumstances.

One day, I decided to wear those Sears jeans with pride, mustering all my confidence. To my surprise, one of the country club girls complimented them. I laughed inside, knowing they were knockoffs. It was at that moment I realized the transformative power of confidence. It can outshine any label and make you feel empowered, no matter the circumstances.

That confidence carried me through a temporary office job where I met JR when I was eighteen. He was not just a boyfriend, but a mentor and a guide. From the moment I saw him, I was smitten. He was twenty years my senior, and his way of thinking was revolutionary. He spoke about the internet in a way I had never heard before, challenging the traditional path for most people—the forty-five-year plan designed to grind you down and leave you with nothing. This resonated deeply with me, having witnessed my parents' struggles.

When JR came into my life, I was at a crossroads. My father, always practical, woke me up one morning insisting that I apply for a flight attendant job at Eastern Airlines. The thought of earning $28,000 a year with seven days off a month felt absurd, especially since I was terrified of flying. But I went to the interview, deliberately giving all the wrong answers, hoping they'd reject me. Instead, I got the job and endured a grueling four-week training program.

Every night, I called my mom in tears, feeling completely out of place. JR, who I had just started dating, became my lifeline. He encouraged me to quit, saying, "If you don't go home and tell your father you're not going to do this, you'll become a version of yourself you won't recognize." His words hit me hard, and I knew he was right. Sometimes the bravest thing you can do is walk away from something not meant for you.

Living Between the Dash

After quitting Eastern Airlines during my training program, I packed my bags and moved in with JR. I hadn't told him my plans beforehand, so when I showed up with my bags, he thought I was crazy. But that moment marked the beginning of our love story and the beginning of living between the dash. JR had encouraged me to stand up to my dad, warning me that if I didn't, I would become someone I didn't want to be. Over the years, I've met countless people who became versions of themselves they never wanted to be, pushed into careers because of someone else's expectations. If I hadn't listened to JR, I could have quickly become one of them, living a life dictated by someone else's dreams instead of my own.

One evening, JR took me on a date I'll never forget. We drove to a cemetery. I was confused, even a little scared. "Why a cemetery?" I asked, looking at him curiously.

He smiled, his eyes reflecting the car's dim interior light. "I want to show you something important," he replied cryptically.

I thought he was a psychopath, crazy, a complete lunatic. But as we walked among the graves, the moon casting long shadows, I began to feel a sense of peace. Finally, JR stopped and pointed at a gravestone. "Look at the dates," he said. "This person was born, lived, and died. That dash in between? That's their entire life."

I stared at the gravestone, the simplicity of the dates hitting me hard. "Living between the dash," he continued, "is what matters. It's what you do in that space that defines you."

Defining My Dash

The next day, I faced my father. "Dad, I'm leaving with JR," I declared, my voice steady despite the storm of emotions inside me. "To build something incredible."

He looked at me, bewildered. "Leaving? With JR? To do what?"

"To build a way for people to shop online."

He shook his head. "That's not even a real thing. You're making a mistake."

But I stood my ground. "I believe in him, and I believe in us. We're going to make it happen."

It was one of the most complex decisions of my life, but also the most liberating. When I decided to leave with JR and pursue our shared vision, we didn't have much, but we had each other. And that was enough. This decision was not just life-changing, it was inspiring, and it led us to where we are today.

Great Love Is Not a Fairy Tale

I can still see him there, standing with that casual confidence, the man who would eventually change my entire life. It's strange how something so monumental can start with such a small, almost insignificant moment. I was mad crazy for JR the second I laid eyes on him. I was young, barely legal, and I saw him at a club in North Carolina. I was used to getting attention back then. I could have danced with anyone I wanted, but JR caught my eye. He was magnetic. Charismatic. Different. And when I asked him to dance, he did something that no one else had done before: he said no.

Not just once—multiple times.

Most men would jump at the chance to dance with me, to be in my space, but not JR. He acted like he didn't even care that I was interested. I remember feeling this rush of confusion and excitement at the same time. Why didn't he want me the way everyone else did? I was intrigued by his nonchalance. He became a puzzle I needed to solve. At first, that's what drew me in so deeply—he was the man who didn't need me the way I was used to being needed.

In hindsight, I understand it was the chase that intrigued me. He was different, removed, as if the room and its inhabitants barely registered in his consciousness. I was accustomed to being the center of attention, the one men gravitated toward, but JR was an enigma, a locked door I was determined to open.

We were in North Carolina then, working for TV Ventures—nothing serious, just a job, not the beginning of an empire. I didn't know where we were headed, but I thought I knew him.

He told me he was divorced. I never thought to question it. Why would I? I was young and in love, or what I thought was love, an all-consuming obsession with how he moved through the world. He was a man who held answers to questions I hadn't yet thought to ask. When he took me to New Jersey for a meeting—something about his latest project, the "As Seen on TV" thing—I thought nothing of it.

But then there was "Brenda Jane."

She was there, in his apartment, like she had always been there. She was older than me, not by much, but enough to feel the weight of it, the way experience drips off a woman like that. I saw the way she looked at him, the half-empty glass of wine in her hand, and I understood something had been broken between us before it ever began.

I wanted to leave. I didn't.

JR called her a friend, but we both knew what that meant. I could see the remnants of their history in how she moved around the apartment, familiar with the space that should have been ours. That night, I wasn't angry. I was disappointed. In myself, in him, in the way things were so easily undone.

Years later, I can see now that moment was the foundation of something bigger than us. It wasn't a fairytale, not even close. But it was real in the way only flawed, broken things can be real. We all carry our ghosts. Brenda Jane was mine, a shadow that lingered in my mind for years, even after JR and I became the power couple everyone saw us as. She was just a spectator, but a painful reminder of how love can unravel, quietly and slowly, until one day you reach a turning point.

JR had to choose—stay in the shadows of the past or step into the light with me. And he chose me. He chose us. That betrayal didn't define our love story, but it shaped it. It forced us to face the hard truths about who we were and what we wanted. It was about choosing to stay because of the love we shared. Our love was worth it. It was worth fighting for. We wanted to make it work. And I believed, in the end, we would have something stronger, a once in a lifetime love.

And we do.

Forgiving What Is Not Forgotten

When I found out about Brenda Jane, I did what most young women do—I told my mother. I expected her to rage on my behalf, to tell me I deserved better, to say the things I didn't dare to believe about myself. Instead, she stayed quiet, too quiet. I remember looking at her, waiting for the flood of maternal anger. But it didn't come. She just nodded as if she'd known all along.

Later, much later, when JR and I had been together for years, after Amber was born, after the business, I learned the truth. My mother had known. She knew he had cheated on me, even back then. She hadn't said anything because she believed in us—in what we could become.

"I didn't want to tell you, Loren," she said, her voice gentle but firm. "I didn't want to interfere because I could see what you two had, what you could build together. Everyone makes mistakes. But I knew JR was the man who would grow into the person you needed him to be."

At the time, I couldn't understand it. How could she know and not tell me? How could she see something in him that I was too hurt to see myself? But now, looking back, I realize she was right. JR and I weren't just about the good times. We were about the work it took to get to the good times. We were about surviving the storms, the moments when everything seemed like it would fall apart, but we didn't.

My mother wasn't just giving us space to figure it out. She was giving me the space to grow into the woman who could weather JR's flaws and for JR to become the man who wouldn't let me down again.

But in those early days, I didn't know any of that. All I knew was that another woman was in his apartment, and I stayed, telling myself that love meant forgiving, even when I wasn't sure if I could.

* * *

Time: Present Day

Subject Line: We're Turning the Corner— Thank You Team

Dear Market America Team,

I'm writing you a quick note of heart-felt gratitude. I want each and every one of you to know how much I appreciate your hard work, dedication, and support. You are the reason we are turning the corner, and I couldn't be more thankful for your contributions to our shared success.

Today, after a grueling tour from January 15 to May 15, 2024, we are finally starting to see the light. Market America has turned a corner and experienced its best growth in the last two months since JR passed away. It's incredible to see us nearing the heights we reached when JR was still here, and I am immensely proud. Our planted seeds are starting to grow, but they still need nurturing, watering, and care. Like anything you want to flourish, you must feed it, give it sunlight, and continuously work on it.

For the first time in almost two years, Market America is beginning to see the light at the end of the tunnel. Things are happening; we're making a difference and working together as a cohesive team. I've had to make tough decisions—changing personnel, letting some go, and pushing others to step up. It's been a rough ride with difficult conversations, but these actions are making a significant impact.

Marc has been a rock and an incredible leader alongside me. Together, we've seen a transformation. While we're not yet where we were before JR passed or COVID hit, we're making steady progress, and that's what matters—constant growth, even if it's slow. JR always said consistent growth is more important than rapid, unprepared expansion that can come crashing down. Our progress is giving me hope.

Marc reminded me just this morning that we both saw the light for the first time in a long time. It's brighter than it's been in twenty-four months.

> And so, with that, another day begins,
> sunny-side up, ready to tackle the
> challenges and continue growing Market
> America beyond its previous heights.
>
> In gratitude, Loren

I was so proud to write this email to my leadership team.

I've been grieving for two years, and the only thing I know to be true is that it changes constantly. Just when you think you've figured out how to control your emotions around it, grief shapeshifts into something new. It's exhausting. After writing the email, I shut my laptop off and let exhaustion take over. It was this night that I had the most peculiar dream.

The Dream: A Visit from Giants

I remember being in a room eerily reminiscent of the waiting room in *Beetlejuice*, where the dead wait to see if they can leave Earth. The walls were a mix of garish lime green and electric purple, adorned with outdated floral wallpaper peeling at the edges. An old-fashioned ticket dispenser stood in the corner, emitting a faint, ghostly glow. The room was filled with the soft murmur of voices, a surreal blend of the ordinary and the bizarre.

"Welcome, Loren," said a woman with a commanding presence and a kind smile. Sheryl Sandberg, Facebook's COO and author of *Lean In*, was seated in an absurdly oversized, plush velvet chair.

I looked around the room and recognized Denise Morrison, the former president and CEO of Campbell Soup Company, who had led the company through significant growth and transformation. Revered *Washington Post* publisher Katharine

Graham was there too, known for her leadership during the Watergate scandal, which cemented her place in history as a pioneer for women in media. Laurene Powell Jobs, the philanthropist and widow of Apple founder Steve Jobs, whose work in education and social justice had made a lasting impact, was also present. They were seated on mismatched chairs that looked like they'd been plucked from a 1970s garage sale, yet somehow, they exuded an air of elegance. I couldn't believe my eyes. "Am I dreaming?" I asked, half expecting someone to pinch me.

"Of course you are," Denise Morrison laughed, adjusting a retro cat-eye monocle. "So, Loren, what's been on your mind?"

I hesitated, feeling both starstruck and vulnerable. "Um. Well, you might have heard that I lost JR about two years ago. It was in the news. Maybe?" I felt like an idiot saying this to these women as if they followed our lives.

Katharine Graham laughed out loud. "Yes, we heard. JR was a big spirit to lose in the world."

"Right! I've been struggling to keep everything together after JR's death. And I'm trying to keep my head above water. The pressure to keep Market America and SHOP.COM growing is immense, and being there for Amber...and the gran...well, I just feel..." I was interrupted.

Laurene Powell Jobs interjected, casually rearranging a model of the solar system that floated midair. "I know *that* feeling. After Steve passed, I felt like I was drowning in expectations. Apple was a massive entity, just like Market America, with countless people relying on its success. I lost Steve only to gain thousands of people I felt responsible for."

Katharine Graham, playing with a tiny typewriter that floated around her head, added quickly, "Yes, exactly! When my husband died, I was thrust into leading the *Washington Post* during some of its most challenging times. The *Pentagon Papers* and Watergate were monumental pressures. I leaned on my instincts and the support of those around me. Like you with Market America, I had to navigate through turbulent waters, but through that chaos, I found my strength."

Sheryl Sandberg smiled warmly, adjusting a giant pair of novelty glasses that magnified her eyes to an absurd size. "Losing Dave was the hardest thing I've ever faced. It made me realize the importance of resilience and the value of my support network. The people I surrounded myself with. Writing *Option B* was part of my healing process, sharing my journey with others who faced similar losses. Getting all the feelings out, not caring who saw them. I was just getting it out. Loren, Market America is a huge organization with a loyal customer base, much like Facebook. The pressure you feel is natural, but it also means you have the opportunity to make a significant impact."

"It's just…so overwhelming. Some days, I feel like I'm barely keeping it together," I admitted.

Denise nodded, balancing a soup can on her head. "That's completely normal. After taking over at Campbell, I faced immense pressure and doubt. But I used that pressure to innovate and drive the company forward. Your situation with SHOP. COM is similar—continuing to innovate and expand can be your path through this."

Laurene said, "Don't forget the absurd moments that keep us grounded. For example, when I was in a board meeting, my phone kept buzzing with texts from my son asking if he could adopt a llama. I had to excuse myself to explain why llamas are not indoor pets."

Katharine chuckled, "Oh, I've had my fair share of those moments. Once, during an important interview, my dog decided it was the perfect time to sing the song of his people. I had to continue, pretending nothing was happening while my colleagues were in stitches."

Denise, still balancing her soup can, chimed in, "Like Laurene said, it's the absurdity of everyday life that keeps us grounded. For example, I accidentally wore two different shoes to a shareholders' meeting. In grief, details get twisted for me. No one noticed, but I laughed about it all day."

Their shared laughter and stories made the weight of my grief feel a little lighter. These women, who had faced unimaginable loss and emerged stronger, reminded me that I, too, could find my way through the storm. I felt a sisterhood with them, even though I knew this sisterhood was a creation of my dream. I was keenly aware I was dreaming but couldn't wake up. Their stories kept me in the dream.

"I turned my focus to meaningful initiatives and continued his legacy. Remember, it's about finding purpose in the chaos," Laurene quipped.

Katharine Graham looked at me with a knowing smile as the dream faded. "You're going to be okay, Loren. You have the strength within you. Just keep swimming."

Living Between the Dash:
The Morning After

I woke up with a jolt, the echo of Katharine's words lingering in my mind. A profound realization settled over me as the morning light filtered through the curtains. These incredible women were living between their dashes—just as JR had shown me all those years ago in the cemetery. They made every moment count, turning their grief into a powerful force for growth and success.

The journey ahead was still daunting, but I felt a kinship with these women who had walked similar paths. Their stories were now a part of mine, guiding me as I navigated the waves of loss and leadership. JR's lesson about living between the dash resonated deeper than ever.

As I got out of bed that morning, I knew one thing: I was determined to live fully between the dash, carrying forward JR's legacy with love, strength, and an unshakeable belief in the power of dreams.

The Lesson: Making Your Dash Count

If there's one thing I've come to understand, both from the remarkable women in my dream and from the wisdom JR imparted, it's this: our lives are not defined by the number of years we have but by how we live the time between the dates— the dash on our gravestones. That dash represents every choice, every challenge, and every moment we have to create meaning— not just for ourselves but for those we love and leave behind.

Grief can be all-consuming. It narrows our focus and makes us feel like the world has reached a standstill. But the truth is, life goes on even in our darkest moments. And it's in these moments—when the pain feels unbearable—we can decide how we want to live our dash.

This meant drawing on the lessons JR taught me to guide Market America through its most challenging times. It meant being there for my family and my team and, most importantly, rediscovering how to be there for myself. I learned that living with purpose doesn't mean ignoring the pain; it means finding a way to move forward because of it.

So here's what I want you to take to heart: No matter who you've lost or how deep your grief is, you can shape your dash. It's okay to feel the pain, to mourn what's gone, but don't let it define the rest of your story. You can choose to let your loss hold you back, or you can choose to let it propel you into a life filled with meaning and purpose.

The journey is challenging—there will be days when it feels like the weight is too much to bear. You might feel like you're barely holding on, and that's okay. Allow yourself those moments, but know this: if you keep moving forward and searching for the light even in the darkest places, you'll discover that life still has so much to offer. There's still joy, love, and purpose waiting to be uncovered.

This is your time, your dash. It's your chance to create a life reflecting the best of who you are and want to become. Don't rush it. Don't pressure yourself to have it all figured out right away. Take it one step at a time, knowing that each step forward, no matter how small, is a victory.

You have the strength within you to live fully, even after loss. Your dash is still being written, and it's entirely up to you how that story unfolds. Make it a story worth telling—one of resilience, courage, and hope.

CHAPTER ELEVEN

MY LOVE LETTER NOW THAT I KNOW

Time: Present Day

My Dearest JR,

I dreamt as a little girl of falling in love with my Prince Charming, who would sweep me off my feet and make my life an endless adventure, just like in those technicolor movies. And then, at eighteen, I met you. Your infectious laughter, your magnetic presence—it all drew me in. Within minutes of our first exchange, I knew I wanted to be part of your life.

There was nothing then—no money, no home, not even a plan. Yet, I believed in you. My intuition knew that being with you was a once-in-a-lifetime opportunity to love deeply and work alongside a creative genius. You stimulated me mentally and mesmerized me with your vision for resurrecting the great American dream.

You dreamed of changing the world, and you did. Watching you build Market America has been incredible. You are brilliant, resilient, and full of purpose. You helped people succeed and inspired them to be their best selves. You didn't just tell a new story—you were the living the dash.

Now, as I sit and write this letter, I realize how much you did the same for me. You gave me confidence, encouraged me when I was unsure, and believed in me when I didn't. You made me realize I am enough. Thank you, baby.

You should know that the world without JR simply makes no sense to me. After you passed, I was drowning in waves of loneliness, sadness, and guilt.

In your absence, I've discovered strength within myself that I never knew existed. To be honest, I've had to reinvent myself because the Loren you knew only made sense when you were directly by my side. I'm figuring out this new Loren, the one who walks through life now, alone but hopeful. I'm imperfect and have learned to let everyone see it. I want to build more and expand more, and just recently I've allowed myself to acknowledge this without feeling bad about the desires.

Grieving with Amber, Ayden, Ayva, Aydrien, and the rest of our family, coupled with taking the reins at Market America, has been the hardest thing I've ever done aside from losing you. I've faced doubt, both from others and within myself. But I've also felt your guiding presence, pushing me forward, reminding me of the strength you always saw in me. I've found my voice, standing on stage with the renewed confidence you always knew I had. Sharing our dreams and vision with the world. I am ready to continue our work, to help others create their dream life, just as we did.

I've learned to stand in my power, to lead with the same clarity, passion, and vision that you did. I've become a softer leader, but with much more clarity and purpose. I'm teaching our team to fall in love, and stay in love, with the small rituals that bind us and not let

171

the grind get in the way. Every decision I make is with you in mind, striving to honor your legacy and continue the work we started together. It's growing, baby. The business will go on and change tens of thousands more lives; I know this to be true.

I've also realized the importance of our family, of rebuilding and nurturing the bonds that keep us strong. Amber and the grandkids have been my anchor, reminding me of the love and joy you brought into our lives. Together, we've navigated the waves of grief, finding more and more moments of happiness and laughter amidst the sorrow. I won't miss a moment of their lives, I promise. And they will live doing the things that burn them up with passion—whatever those things are.

Every day, I am reminded of how deeply you are missed by thousands of people whose lives you touched.

The letters I receive from all over the world speak of one thing consistently: how you empowered them to believe in themselves. You had a unique gift, JR. You saw potential in people and made them see it too. I see now how many others you inspired.

Your absence has left a void, but your legacy of empowerment lives on. The seeds you planted in so many hearts continue to grow, and I promise you, I am doing everything I can to nurture them. I will keep dreaming for both of us. And when my time comes, I know you'll be waiting for me in Heaven, ready to continue our journey together.

Thank you for being you. For your heart, your love, your life. For showing us what life looks like when you live the dash. I was right about you at eighteen—you are my once-in-a-lifetime opportunity. I fell, kept falling, and am still falling madly in love with you more than three decades later. Every love story is beautiful, but ours is my favorite. I promise you—there will be more magic moments.

If I knew then what I know now, I would have written you this love letter and left it for you to find one morning as you stepped out of the shower. To read before you shared coffee with me. You wrote me over 5,600 love letters, and I saved them all. But this is the letter I could only have written, now, after I know who I am without JR.

And the answer finally hit me, baby.
Always sunny-side up—in breakfast and
life.

I love you—forever. I believe in you.
And I believe in me, finally.

Yours always,
Loren

A Gift in the Aftermath

The letter I found in JR's email drafts folder, an email never sent, was a gift from heaven almost two years after his death.

Your life and the journey you have made,
as well as what you have become, are a
shining beacon of light, love, success,
accomplishment, graciousness, sensitiv-
ity, and enlightenment. You're living
life to the fullest for your family,
friends, and thousands of women, UFOs,
and entrepreneurs that see you as a role
model. Your life has become a monument
to what love, success, and dreams are
about. I am so proud of you and honored
to be your soulmate, best friend, and
partner in life, love, and business. It
is hard to believe that the years have
flown by, and we have reached a milestone
in living. You have spent over half
your life with me, and I hope you can
look back and marvel at the miraculous

journey we have been on, smile, and feel some satisfaction. I believe we have done well, and we look forward to the greatest chapter of that journey together. We will experience and accomplish the remaining missions we have set in our lives together. I am so proud of who you have become. We have always had a purpose, and life without one is not worth living. You have always been a beautiful, sexy, stunning girl from the moment we met, and now a gorgeous, sexy woman. But no one knows, like I know, how much more beautiful you are inside. You are the most amazing person I have ever met, and I have been so blessed to have our paths and lives collide and merge into one. We have accomplished almost everything we set out to achieve, and now all I want you to do is enjoy your success, family, time, and life as you have given our life your all and deserve the very best that life allows one to experience on this earth. My gift to you is to make your life what you deserve and want it to be our journey and forever more. Today is the first day of the rest of your life; I hope it is a happy one and the beginning of a new chapter and the best chapter of a long, turbulent, exciting, and triumphant love story.

Love, JR

CHAPTER TWELVE

CARRYING THE FLAME

IT WAS ICON 2024, MARKET America's largest event of the year. I stood in a stadium filled with five thousand people, smaller than our past eighteen thousand attendees, but a number that continued to grow after the end of the COVID shutdown. The lights were blinding as I stepped onto the stage. The energy was electric, almost palpable, yet this time, it felt different. JR wasn't beside me, and the void he left was something I carried with me every single day. But here I was, standing in front of thousands of people who needed me to be strong and to lead. This was the moment JR had prepared me for—this responsibility, this challenge. And so, I stepped forward.

"Two people can build a team," I began, my words intense, intentional. "Two by two by two by two. But what do you think a group like us can do for the world?"

I paused, letting the question hang in the air. I could feel them with me, leaning in, waiting for what came next. This wasn't just a speech—it was a challenge, a call to arms.

"If two people can build a team, an organization, what can we do as a group for the nation, for the globe?" I continued, feeling the fire ignite in my chest. "Who cares about the election? Do you care about what happens in November?"

The crowd murmured, unsure of where I was going. I saw their confusion and hesitation, and it fueled me.

"I don't give a shit," I said, the words coming out sharper than I intended, but I didn't care. "What I care about is you becoming the president of your life. You're in charge. You are in charge right there—yes, in the third row. Every single one of you, you're in charge. No president in any country is going to change your life. The only person who can change your life is you."

The silence in the stadium was heavy, but it was the kind of silence that told me they were getting it. They understood what I was saying and felt its weight.

"My grandchildren know they can do anything," I continued, softening my tone and letting them into my world. Ayva, Aydrien, Ayden, as well as my nieces Violet, Mariah, Bria, Layla, and nephews Mekai, Hunter, and Tobias, all sitting in the front row, looked up at me, smiling, beaming. "Anything is possible. Nothing is impossible. You have to teach that now, today. Our children, our grandchildren—they look to us. We have to show them the way."

I scanned the faces in the crowd, seeing the recognition and understanding. This wasn't just about making money or building a business. It was about life, about what we leave behind.

Returning to the Girl Who Didn't Know Better

"When you can get comfortable being uncomfortable," I continued, my voice strong but tender, "you can have anything you want. Life can be suffering. But here's the secret: find something that's worth suffering for, and go get it. Because life without growth isn't life at all, is it? A life without growth is just existence. And we weren't meant to just exist—we were meant to thrive."

I paused, letting that truth sink in, the weight of it settling over the room like a blanket. "We can change ourselves. We are built to endure, to adapt, and to make life fit into our beliefs. But to change your world, your story has to change. You have to change. Stop surrounding yourself with people who don't challenge you, who let you stay comfortable in mediocrity. Stop letting others' doubts become your own. If you let that happen, you've already lost the battle."

I could feel the tension building in the room, the understanding dawning in their eyes. "You have to decide—right now—whether you're going to step forward or step back. If you're not going to go for it, if you're not willing to give it everything you've got, then nothing else matters. Your opinion, your fears, your doubts—they don't matter. What matters is that you show up."

But even as I said those words, I knew I needed to address the darker side, the part of my journey I hadn't been ready to face for so long.

A Mirror and a Choice

"I need to be honest with you," I continued, my voice softening. "When I lost JR, I lost more than my husband. I lost my anchor, my biggest supporter, the man who saw something in me before I ever saw it in myself. And I'll tell you the truth—after he died, I went back to being that unsure girl he met all those years ago. The one who didn't know what self-confidence could do to change a life. I was lost, stuck in a world of guilt, self-doubt, and acceptance of things as they were, rather than how they should be."

I could feel the tears welling up, but I pushed forward, knowing this was the moment of truth. "For so long, I was trapped in the belief that I was connected to everything that had happened to me—the loss, the pain, the heartache—instead of being connected to what I could still achieve, regardless of that loss. I was so focused on everything I had lost that I forgot to be grateful for everything I had lived with JR. I forgot that even though I lost my greatest love, I still had more love to give, more work to do, more lives to touch."

The tears were falling now, but I didn't wipe them away. I let them stay, let the audience see the raw emotion that was as much a part of my journey as the successes. "I'm calling myself out right here, right now," I said, my voice cracking but steady. "It took me too long to realize that. I was wallowing in what was gone, instead of living for what was still here. And I'm telling you—if you're stuck in that place, in that mindset, it's time to wake up. It's time to stop mourning what you've lost and start loving what you still have. It's time to love harder than ever before because that's what makes it all worth it."

179

A Promise Kept

There's a memory that keeps replaying in my mind. It's one of those quiet moments that didn't seem important at the time, but now, it's everything. It was late, long after the conference calls and meetings had ended. JR and I were sitting in our living room, the hum of the city outside our windows, but inside, it was just the two of us.

"Loren," he said, his voice soft, almost tender. "There's going to come a day when you'll have to do this without me."

I looked at him, the words not sinking in. "Don't say that," I replied, brushing it off. "We're a team. We'll always be a team."

He smiled that knowing smile he had when he was about to drop some serious wisdom. "We are a team," he agreed. "But I need you to promise me something."

"What?" I asked, feeling a knot form in my stomach.

"When that day comes, when it's just you, promise me you won't stop. Promise me you'll keep pushing, keep leading. The world needs you, Loren. Our family needs you. Market America needs you."

I didn't want to hear it. I didn't want to think about a world without him. But I nodded, my throat tight. "I promise," I whispered. I promise. I promise.

Now, standing on this stage, that promise is all I can think about. JR isn't here, but his belief in me, his confidence, is. And I'm not going to let him down.

I took a deep breath, feeling the energy shift in the room, the understanding that we were all in this together. "I'm challenging you right now," I continued, my voice gaining strength. "I'm challenging you to look in the mirror and ask yourself—what am I doing with my life? Am I loving enough? Am I serving enough? Am I giving everything I have? Because that's what it takes. That's what it takes to live a life of meaning, to leave a legacy worth remembering."

The crowd was electric now, the emotion thick in the air. This was more than just a speech; it was a call to action. "It's time to rise above the chaos," I urged them. "It's time to rise above the fear, the doubt, the guilt. It's time to rise above everything that's holding you back and step into the light of what you're meant to be. You've got one life—one chance to make it count. Don't you waste it."

I could see the determination on their faces, the resolve to take this message to heart and make it their own. "Life is too short to live with regrets," I said, my voice firm. "Too short to wonder what could have been. Don't let your dreams die with you. The world is waiting for you to step into your greatness. What are you willing to do to become all you were meant to be?"

The crowd was on their feet now, the energy explosive, ready to take on the world. "How far are you willing to go?" I challenged them. "How hard are you willing to fight? The time is now. Don't wait for tomorrow because tomorrow is not promised. Live for today. Love for today. Serve for today. Because that's what makes it all worth it."

As I stepped back, the applause thundered through the stadium, the energy surging like a wave. I knew in that moment that JR was with me, proud of the journey I had taken, the woman I had become. And I knew that together, we had inspired a movement, a legion of people ready to rise above their fears and their doubts, and step into greatness.

The Lesson: Create Your Best Life

I need you to understand something that's taken me two years to grasp. Losing JR was the hardest thing I've ever gone through. It shattered me and brought me to my knees in a way I didn't think was possible. But here's the thing—I'm still standing. I'm still here, still fighting, still leading.

Because that's what JR would have wanted; that's what he taught me. Life isn't about avoiding pain or loss but finding your best life despite it. It's about taking the love, lessons, and wisdom from those we've lost and using them to fuel our journey forward.

So, if you're out there struggling, feeling like you can't go on—know that you can. You have the strength within you to overcome anything. You have the power to be the president of your life, take control, lead, love, and build something beautiful, even in the face of unimaginable loss.

This chapter isn't just about me. It's about all of us. It's about finding our best life after losing our greatest love. It's about honoring those before us by living fully, boldly, and purposefully. It's about showing up, even when it's hard, and shining anyway.

So, let's do this. Together. Let's make ourselves proud. Let's find our best life—because we deserve nothing less.

The Giant Hamster Wheel

JR demonstrated this year after year at every conference. "Most of us are on a giant hamster wheel going nowhere fast, doing the same thing over and over again and not making progress. In order to succeed, you're going to have to get off the wheel."

**Anything Is Possible When You
Get Out of Your Comfort Zone**
(26th Conference, circa 2018)

Getting people out of their comfort zone was one of the greatest
lessons he shared with people, and he did it with his own grandchildren from a young age. Here, JR was demonstrating with our
oldest grandson, Ayden, that anything is possible—in front of a
crowd of fifteen thousand people. More importantly, JR believed in
raising young people to believe in themselves and have confidence at
a young age. Ayden was nervous, but look at his face! (I loved that
Ayden was giving everyone a thumbs-up, and the people in the arena
were standing and taking photos!) When he and Pop Pop stepped
out of the capsule, he was so excited and wanted to do it again!

Enjoying Every Moment
(20th convention, circa 2012)

This was one of JR's favorite pictures, watching and learning from people on stage and enjoying every moment of it!

What Are You Going to Do with The Dash?
(30th convention, circa 2022)

The date that you're born and the date that you die don't matter. What matters in life is what you do with the time in between—"The Dash." JR shared this at every conference. If you do something with The Dash, you'll never leave life with regrets. What are you going to do with your dash? That is all that matters, and sharing this was so important to him.

185

Our Wedding Day
(December 11, 1996, Barbados)

Such an incredible day. I was marrying the love
of my life. We were both so happy!

Our Market America Team
(circa 1993)

What is so amazing about this picture is our team has never changed; we have stayed together all these years. We've accomplished so much together and yet we're just beginning.

JR Would Light Up Every Time They Were Around
(circa 2018)

JR loves his family! His face would always light up when they were around. Here he is with our daughter, Amber, and grandchildren Aydrien, Ayva, and Ayden.

Our Last Picture Together
(August 30, 2022, Croatia, one hour before JR passed away)

He looked perfectly healthy. We were so happy
to get away. We deserved a break. I never thought
that this would be our last photo together.

ABOUT THE AUTHOR

LOREN RIDINGER IS A VISIONARY entrepreneur, philanthropist, and global influencer, renowned as the co-founder and CEO of Market America Worldwide and SHOP.COM, an award-winning global e-commerce and digital marketing company. Over the past three decades, she and her late husband, JR Ridinger, have transformed Market America into a billion-dollar enterprise, empowering thousands to achieve financial independence through the revolutionary UnFranchise® Business model, paying out over $6 billion to its entrepreneurial base, cementing its role as a life-changing platform for aspiring entrepreneurs.

A digital innovator, Loren has launched multiple successful brands in beauty, health, wellness, and personal care, creating high-quality products that resonate with consumers worldwide. Her commitment to excellence has not only transformed lives but also inspired countless entrepreneurs to pursue their own success stories.

Loren's influence extends beyond the business realm. She is a passionate philanthropist, actively supporting initiatives that empower women and children, including her work with the Make-A-Wish Foundation. Her dedication to uplifting communities reflects her commitment to making a lasting impact.

As a respected thought leader and sought-after speaker, Loren shares her insights on entrepreneurship and personal growth with hundreds of thousands, inspiring people around the globe to lead empowered, purposeful lives. Her story is one of resilience and unwavering dedication, continuing to inspire a new generation of entrepreneurs while driving meaningful change worldwide.

In addition to her professional accomplishments, Loren is a proud mother to her daughter, Amber, and a loving Mimi to three grandchildren: Ayden, Ayva, and Aydrien.